God Yes? God No?

God Yes? God No?

The Answer from Science

FRANS KÖMHOFF

RESOURCE *Publications* • Eugene, Oregon

GOD YES? GOD NO?
The Answer from Science

Copyright © 2024 Frans Kömhoff. All rights reserved. Except for brief quotations in critical publications or reviews, no part of this book may be reproduced in any manner without prior written permission from the publisher. Write: Permissions, Wipf and Stock Publishers, 199 W. 8th Ave., Suite 3, Eugene, OR 97401.

Resource Publications
An Imprint of Wipf and Stock Publishers
199 W. 8th Ave., Suite 3
Eugene, OR 97401

www.wipfandstock.com

PAPERBACK ISBN: 979-8-3852-1253-8
HARDCOVER ISBN: 979-8-3852-1254-5
EBOOK ISBN: 979-8-3852-1255-2

06/18/24

Figures 15 and 19 by Daniël Maas

All other graphical illustrations by Paul Scholte

Various images have been taken from Wikimedia Commons. As a token of gratitude, the author has made a donation to the Wikimedia Foundation.

Scripture quotations marked (NIV) are taken from the Holy Bible, New International Version®, NIV®. Copyright © 1973, 1978, 1984, 2011 by Biblica, Inc.™ Used by permission of Zondervan. All rights reserved worldwide. www.zondervan.com The "NIV" and "New International Version" are trademarks registered in the United States Patent and Trademark Office by Biblica, Inc.™

Scripture quotations taken from the (NASB®) New American Standard Bible®, Copyright © 1960, 1971, 1977, 1995 by The Lockman Foundation. Used by permission. All rights reserved. lockman.org

For Eera

> Whatever knowledge is attainable, must be attained by scientific methods; and what science cannot discover, mankind cannot know.
>
> —Bertrand Russell

Contents

Introduction		ix
Acknowledgments		xiii
1	Proof of God	1
2	A Quick Look at Religion	10
3	Considering Philosophy	22
4	And Then There Was Life	30
5	The Accidental Universe	38
6	The Ascension of the Spirit	43
7	The Body-Spirit Issue	46
8	Answering the Big Questions	54
9	The End of the Universe	64
10	The Future of the Universe	71
To Close		75
Appendix 1: Isaac Newton		79
Appendix 2: Charles Darwin		85
Appendix 3: Albert Einstein		92
Appendix 4: Quantum Physics		108
Appendix 5: Stephen Hawking		129
Glossary		139
Sources of Illustrations		147
Bibliography		151
Index		157

Introduction

THIS BOOK IS, IN essence, an extrapolation of what great minds of the past have come up with. Icons that have been decisive for the progress of science, natural science in particular. I'll mention a few names you'll know: Isaac Newton, Charles Darwin, Albert Einstein, and Stephen Hawking. And of course, I mustn't forget the various founders of quantum physics, scientists like Max Planck, Niels Bohr, and many others. Most of them have already passed away, but there's a new generation of great minds ready to continue their work.

One might rightly ask what the role of natural science is in answering metaphysical questions. The answer to this is simple: none at all! Natural science cannot and doesn't want to answer questions as whether God exists or not. However, we can evaluate claims attributed to God that fall within the realm of natural science, on their scientific merits, and approve or disprove them on that basis.

Philosophers have been debating the existence or nonexistence of God for more than 2,600 years, but they actually haven't made much progress. Nevertheless, I will include what philosophy has taught us, because many great thinkers have developed ideas that might be valuable for my story—for example, about the body-mind issue, which is relevant for my analysis of religions.

I'll tell my story as simply as possible, using as few mathematical formulas as possible as these tend to put people off! That's a shame because formula phobia is actually unfounded. For the physicist, a mathematical formula is the epitome of beauty because

Introduction

it's the most compact format to even summarize an entire theory. Look at perhaps the best-known formula of all: $E = mc^2$. It's not that complex—with a little imagination, you could even argue that mathematical formulas are the "black holes" in the cosmos of knowledge.

In this book, I'm going to examine three religions, namely Judaism, Christianity, and Islam, looking at these three criteria:

- How does natural science view these religions?
- Can truth be derived from oral and written tradition?
- Which contradictions can be found based on logic?

Given the limited scope of this book, it's inevitable that I'll have to rush through these subjects with great strides while trying to capture their essence. To make sense of the underlying theories, I've included a summary of each of them in the appendices, as well as a brief description of their discoverers. You don't need to read these appendices, but for example, if you want to understand how natural selection works, read appendix 2: "Charles Darwin." If you want to understand why time didn't exist before the big bang, read appendix 3: "Albert Einstein." Knowledge of Isaac Newton's classical mechanics (appendix 1) will help you place Einstein's theory in the right perspective. To learn more about the "theory of everything," some understanding of quantum physics (appendix 4) is inevitable. If you want to understand black holes, go to appendix 5: "Stephen Hawking." In fact, you can view these appendices as a crash course in the relevant theories. I think that a basic understanding of these theories will help you grasp the essence of the origin and evolution of both the universe and humanity. And, to help you with some commonly used terms, I've added a glossary.

My narrative is larded with personal reflections that sometimes go beyond the scope of this book, with a lighthearted note here and there. After all, the underlying material is tough enough. If I hurt any reader's feelings with what I've written, I apologize; this was never my intention.

Introduction

Then, to finish, I'm not trying to force my beliefs on anyone, and I only want to tell my own story, based on today's scientific knowledge. However, if you catch me making factual inaccuracies, I'd greatly appreciate it if you'd let me know, via my publisher, so that I can correct things in the next edition.

Acknowledgments

I AM GRATEFUL TO the following persons, who have reviewed all or part of the manuscript and have provided useful comments:

Peter Barratt-Jones

Ton Bertels

Pieter-Jan Brouwer

Roy Erkens

Theo van Es

Yannick Fritschy

Ben Geerts

Sjef Geevers

Bert Gelderblom

Serge Lamar

Piet Meulendijks

Herman Philipse

Leon Piatkowski

Vincent Sanders

Frank Steller

Of course, the ultimate responsibility for the final text rests entirely with myself.

1

Proof of God

FROM TIME IMMEMORIAL, WE humans have looked at the cosmos and have been so impressed by the grandeur of the firmament that we've concluded that a creator must be needed for this wonder. Again, through time, scientists have examined the microcosm through their microscopes and have been equally impressed by its beauty, also coming to a similar conclusion.

From these thoughts, the so-called intelligent design movement was born. Supporters claim that the complexity of nature can only be explained by the existence of an intelligent designer. They're like the ancient Greeks, who created a "god" for any phenomenon they couldn't otherwise explain. However, the intelligent design argument is a pseudo-god proof that doesn't hold up scientifically.

In principle, natural science isn't concerned with answers to metaphysical questions like the existence or non-existence of God. What natural science can do, however, is evaluate metaphysical statements that fall within its domain using a scientific approach. And that's exactly what we're going to do in this book.

If God himself had ever visited the earth and this had been established by objective observation, this would provide evidence for God's existence. A possible verification could be when Moses spoke to God on Mount Sinai and received the two tablets containing the Ten Commandments. Reportedly, both tablets were not only made by God, but also inscribed by his finger.

Unknown artist
Figure 1. Moses breaking the two tablets.

Had we been able to trace these tablets, we could possibly, with the latest DNA techniques, have traced DNA material from God. Unfortunately, when Moses descended from Mount Sinai, he broke the stone tablets when he saw his people worshiping the golden calf. Furthermore, Moses provided no other tangible evidence, so we can only take him at his word. And, by the way, this is also true for the Prophet Muhammad regarding his meeting with the archangel Gabriel, who whispered the texts of the Qur'an to him. Unfortunately, one person's account of seeing or hearing something is too narrow a basis to serve as generally acceptable evidence. Had it been conclusively established at the time that God really did exist, our history would have taken a very different turn—and probably a less violent one.

What Does History Tell Us?

In pre-Christian times, stories were passed on orally, and this went on for centuries, from around 1800 BC in the time of the patriarch Abraham, from generation to generation.

Obviously, it's difficult to establish truth from this long chain of oral tradition. Later on, the story of the life of Jesus was recorded by the four evangelists Matthew, John, Mark, and Luke. There are also written traditions known from the enemy camp of the Romans, and their version doesn't contradict those of the Bible. Keeping in mind the journalistic principle of adversarial debate, there's scholarly agreement that around the beginning of our era, a figure called Jesus may have walked around Israel surrounded by a number of followers. However, the actions of Jesus Christ are interpreted differently by everyone. But that's also true these days—cults and cult leaders are of all times.

Proof of God Based on Logic

Several attempts have been made throughout history to prove that God exists by logical reasoning. Let's examine a few.

Unknown artist

St. Anselm of Canterbury (1033–1109)

St. Anselm was an Italian philosopher, a theologian, and a devout Christian, witnessed by his statement: "For I do not seek to understand in order to believe, but I believe in order to understand. For I believe this: unless I believe, I will not understand."[1] Anselm is considered the founder of scholasticism, the church intelligentsia in the late Middle Ages. Anselm believed that the Bible was not convincing enough to win over nonbelievers. Therefore, he devised a way to explain God from reason. Anselm is best known for his ontological proof of God. This reads as follows:

1. God is the most perfect thing we can imagine.
2. Existence is more perfect than nonexistence.
3. Ergo, God exists.

---

1. Bromiley, *Historical Theology*, 172.

Proof of God

It is striking that Anselm started from the premise that God exists, when in fact he had to prove it. The philosopher Immanuel Kant (1724–1804) rejected Anselm's proof of God in his *Kritik der reinen Vernunft* on the basis of his view that "existence" is not a property and that "existence" cannot be more perfect than "nonexistence."

Carlo Crivelli, 1476

Thomas Aquinas (1225–1274)

Thomas Aquinas, an Italian philosopher and theologian, was one of the most influential thinkers in medieval scholasticism. He produced five "proofs" of God—the "Five Ways"—by which one could arrive at God.[2] The first and most famous way, that of the "First Mover," is based on the principle of cause and effect. It should be

2. Kenny, *Five Ways*.

noted that Thomas was not the originator of the concept of the First Mover, but Aristotle. Thomas merely built on it to prove the existence of God. His reasoning is as follows: nothing in our sensory world moves by itself and must therefore be moved by something. That something must in turn also be moved by something else, and so on. But, Thomas argues, you cannot go on like this indefinitely and therefore there must be a very first mover. This First Mover or Unmoved Mover will be understood by all to be God.

Even if there were such a being as the Unmoved Mover, it would not necessarily equal God. Various philosophers, e.g., Immanuel Kant (1724–1804) and David Hume (1711–1776), have rejected Thomas Aquinas's proof of God for other reasons. With present-day knowledge, we know that in the quantum world, phenomena can indeed occur without an identifiable cause.

After Frans Hals, 1649–1700

René Descartes (1596–1650)

French philosopher and mathematician René Descartes was the founder of rationalism, which ushered in the period of the

Enlightenment. He is also called the "father of modern philosophy." To summarize, Descartes assumes that man's thinking is closed, and therefore finite. That's why the idea of infinity cannot come from man himself but must have an origin outside man. This origin would then have to be God. While Descartes draws a quasi-logical conclusion from a metaphysical premise, the premise itself is questionable, to say the least.

Unknown artist, ca. 1665

Baruch Spinoza (1632–1677)

Baruch Spinoza, a Dutch-Jewish philosopher, is considered one of the founding fathers of the Enlightenment. He advocated freedom of religion and speech, as well as a strict separation of church and state. Spinoza reasoned as follows: "Inability to exist is impotence, and, on the other hand, ability to exist is power, as is self-evident. If, therefore, there is nothing which necessarily exists excepting things finite, it follows that things finite are more powerful than the absolute infinite Being, and this (as self-evident) is absurd; therefore either nothing exists or Being absolutely infinite also necessarily exists. Therefore the Being absolutely infinite, that is to say, God, necessarily exists."[3]

In this proof of God, Spinoza states *a priori* that an absolutely infinite being exists. Some philosophers call this, euphemistically, an axiomatic proof, which is to say that it is no proof at all. Spinoza, incidentally, had a particular view of God. According to him, there is no creator God; his God is omnipresent in nature. Clearly, Spinoza was a pantheist.

Common to all these philosophers was that they were deeply religious. Apparently, it is difficult to build neutral, independent reasoning with this extreme belief.

Several proofs of God take the form of a syllogism. First, here's an example of a correct syllogism:

1. Socrates is a human being;
2. All humans are mortal;
3. Socrates is mortal.

Syllogistic proofs of God are often read, in terms of content, as follows:

1. All humans are mortal;
2. Immortality is a higher quality than mortality;
3. A being immortal therefore exists, namely God.

Here, there are three logical errors in the same syllogism.

Many other proofs of God exist, but on balance, they all turn out to be either tautologies or circular arguments or fallacies. In this respect, there's not much to be expected in future either.

Thought Experiment

However, there's still one small glimmer of hope for a highly unlikely, hypothetical event, namely the following. We cannot rule out that other life exists elsewhere in the universe, beings perhaps

---

3. Craig, *Cosmological Argument*, 241–42.

far more intelligent than us. If so, it's conceivable that, by now, these extraterrestrials may have captured images of Moses meeting God on Mount Sinai with their telescopes. This, of course, depends on how far away these beings are. And when they are, or have been, kind enough to transmit these images to the earth, at any moment, our telescopes could receive a YouTube video starring God. This then empirically would resolve the question of whether or not God exists in one fell swoop. Unfortunately, the same cannot be done for archangel Gabriel, who, 1,250 years after Moses, appeared to the Prophet Muhammad in a cave! Therefore, the light of this encounter has never reached the outside world.

Now that apparently the so-called proofs of God offer no basis on which to build, we have no choice but to continue our search to trace those events in the creation and development of our universe that could have taken place without God's interference. Let's therefore examine the origin and development of our universe from a natural science point of view. But first, we'll make a brief critical foray into religion and philosophy.

2

A Quick Look at Religion

Judaism, Christianity, and Islam are also called the Abrahamic religions due to the fact that all three recognize the patriarch Abraham as their progenitor. However, a widespread misunderstanding is that they also recognize one and the same God. Jews and Christians do not recognize the Prophet Muhammad, and therefore neither Allah nor the Qur'an. Muslims, in turn, recognize that while Jesus was a prophet, they do not believe he was the Son of God. The Jews do not recognize Jesus as the messiah; in fact, they do not recognize the Trinity and, according to them, the messiah is yet to come. Let's critically review each religion separately.

CHRISTIANITY

Let me start with a brief version of the creation story according to the Old Testament book of Genesis:

On day one: In the beginning God created the heavens and the earth. Then he spoke, "Let there be light." And there was light. So, God created the light and separated the light from the darkness; the light he called the day; the darkness he called the night. However, the Bible doesn't actually mention the source of that light! According to the big bang story, it took at least one hundred million years for the first stars to form. Until then, the universe was shrouded in darkness. The sun was formed more than nine billion years after the big bang. Only thereafter could the sun's light radiate across the earth. But let me stop here to criticize the biblical creation story.

On day two: God spoke, "Let there be a firmament." And immediately the blue firmament showed itself.

On day three: God separated the water from the earth, and plants and trees appeared.

On day four: God created the sun, the moon, and the stars.

On day five: God commanded that "fish swim in the water, and birds fly in the sky." And God saw that it was good.

On day six: God said, "Let the earth bring forth all kinds of animals."[1] And so it was done. Then God created man in his image and likeness.

And finally, on day seven: God rested, and he blessed and sanctified this day.

So the very first sentence in the Bible already clashes head-on with natural science, which says that the universe, including the earth, came into being from the big bang. For centuries, the church and natural science have been at odds, often hostile, because the results of natural science conflicted with those of the biblical creation story. The Catholic Church, centrally directed from Rome, was always ready to comment on crucial world events. However, this wasn't true for the Jewish religion and Islam. So, let's begin to consider some of the major paradigm shifts in natural science and look at the Roman Catholic Church's response to them.

---

1. Bible passages taken from Mes, *Bijbelsche Geschiedenis*.

J. Falck, seventeenth century

Nicolaus Copernicus (1473–1543)

From the beginning of our era, the church was the most powerful institution in society, both in a spiritual and material sense. Until late in the Middle Ages, people believed that the earth was flat and the center of the universe, in accordance with the biblical creation story. However, it was the Renaissance polymath and Catholic canon, the Pole Nicolaus Copernicus, who introduced the heliocentric model around 1532, stating that not the earth but the sun is the center of the universe, and that the planets circle around it.[2] This position was diametrically opposed to the church's view of the earth, which had been motionless since ancient Greece, and was the center of the universe. Copernicus came to his revolutionary idea by imagining he was standing on the sun. From this position, he could explain the revolutions of the heavenly bodies better than from his position on earth. His theory was noticed in Rome and Copernicus was invited to the Vatican Council as an astronomer, but he didn't dare go, afraid

2. Copernicus, *On the Revolutions*.

that because of his cosmological views, he would fall out of favor with the Pope. It was only years later, in the year of his death in 1543, that his book *On the Revolutions of the Heavenly Spheres* was published. In 1616, it was placed on the Papal Index of banned books. For proclaiming the ideas of Copernicus, Italian philosopher Giordano Bruno (1548-1600) was sentenced to be burned at the stake on the authority of the church.[3] On 17 February 1600, his sentence was carried out. His books were also added to the list. The Italian physicist Galileo Galilei (1564-1642) continued to publicly defend Copernicus's work; in particular the thesis that the earth itself moves led to the intervention of church authorities.[4] In 1633, Galilei was sentenced by the Inquisition to house arrest for the rest of his days.

Juliet Margaret Camaron, 1869

Charles Darwin (1809-1882)

Charles Darwin is the creator of the theory of evolution. He discovered that organisms, in their struggle for existence, that are best

---

3. Maifreda, *Trial of Giordano Bruno*.
4. Scotti, *Galileo Revisited*.

adapted to their environment or changing conditions ensure their best chances of survival. He called this process "natural selection." He further observed that in all species, certain favorable traits were passed on to offspring. He also concluded that all life on earth should have a common ancestor. He described his theory in his famous book *On the Origin of Species,* but it took Darwin twenty years before he dared publish as he was aware that it conflicted with the biblical version of creation. The church's reaction was, of course, predictable. The proposition that an animal soul could develop into a human soul was totally unacceptable. The church was also afraid that Darwinism could lead to materialism and atheism.

Unknown photographer

Gregor Mendel (1822-1884)

A contemporary of Darwin was the Czech Gregor Mendel, a monk in the Augustinian order and discoverer of the laws of heredity. Mendel began experimenting with crossing edible peas in his monastery garden and deduced the statistical relationships that form the basis for the science of genetics. Charles Darwin and Gregor Mendel are now considered the fathers of modern biology.

A Quick Look at Religion

Mendel's discoveries, however, were so revolutionary at the time, that the church ordered all his scientific work to be burned.[5]

Unknown photographer, 1933

Georges Lemaître (1894–1966)

Georges Lemaître was a Belgian Catholic priest as well as a genius astrophysicist and mathematician. He became inspired after meeting the American astrophysicist Edwin Hubble (1889–1953) who had concluded from his cosmic observations that the universe is expanding, and the further galaxies are from us, the faster they are moving away from us. Lemaître basically started to play this cosmic movie backward, reasoning as follows: if the universe is ever-expanding, then it must have been ever-smaller in the past, going back to a starting point with an enormously compact mass. That mass he called the "primeval atom." On 19 May 1931, the *New York Times* headlined, "Lemaître Suggests One, Single, Great Atom, Embracing All Energy, Started the Universe." Also according to him, time would start on "the day without yesterday." Later

---

5. Mendel, *Experiments in Plant Hybridization*.

this theory became known as the big bang theory. After his discovery, Lemaître kept his theory under wraps for about a decade, fearing it would bring him into conflict with Rome. When he was finally summoned by Pope Pius XII, he traveled to Rome with a heavy heart. To his great surprise, however, the Pope reacted elatedly for he assumed that the big bang was God's creation moment. This time, a paradigm shift in views on the origin of our universe did not lead to a storm of protests from Rome, on the contrary.

The Catholic Crisis

We have now reached the present day, and we see the Catholic Church in deep crisis with a low number of seminarians, endangering the church's function and future. Churches have lost their congregations and the buildings are being converted into residential units or event halls. In 2022, there were only about a dozen Dutch seminarians still in training, with students mostly being recruited from abroad, especially from India. In this sense, the Netherlands themselves have become a mission country. There are proposals to make priesthood more attractive by, for example, abolishing celibacy, but this is still a step too far for conservative Rome. Moreover, the Catholic Church has increasingly had to respond to the huge media attention regarding the scandals around the problem of abusive priests. It's difficult to imagine what's going on in the mind of an abusive priest when he sees his reflection in a mirror. Surely he must realize that his chances of entering eternity have been drastically reduced by his own doing. Of course, abusive Roman Catholic priests have an escape route, in the form of the sacrament of confession, laundering their souls with a few prayers. There's a good chance that an abusive priest will find (or deliberately seek out) an abusive confessor in the confessional who will then grant him absolution. But outside the Catholic Church there's no reset possible, and it's inevitable that non-Catholic abusive priests must prosecute their lives with a gigantic moral conflict. All things considered, I cannot help feeling that the history of the Catholic Church is becoming increasingly like the rise and fall of the Roman Empire.

A Quick Look at Religion

ISLAM

Islam, a relatively young religion, originated around AD 610 when the archangel Gabriel (Arabic: Djibriel) appeared to the Prophet Muhammad in a cave in Mount Hira, near Mecca. Allah is said to have transmitted the Qur'an in the form of verses (Arabic: *soeras*), through the archangel Gabriel, indirectly to Muhammad. This transmission took place over a period of about twenty-three years, in different places in Arabia. Communication was always in Arabic: "Islam" means submission in Arabic, "Allah" means *the God*, and "Qur'an" means recitation. The world's two billion Muslims are required to read or recite the Qur'an in Arabic; a translation is considered inauthentic. Allah apparently is monolingual!

Rashid-al-Din Hamadani, 1306-1315
Figure 2. Muhammad receiving his first revelation from the archangel Gabriel.

The verses of the Qur'an undeniably contain passages considered as violent, but this is also true for passages in the Bible. Some examples:

> Now go and strike Amalek and utterly destroy all that he has, and do not spare him; but put to death both man

> and woman, child and infant, ox and sheep, camel and donkey. (1 Sam 15:3 NASB)
>
> Their little ones also will be dashed to pieces before their eyes; their houses will be plundered, and their wives ravished. (Isa 13:16 NASB)
>
> Utterly slay old men, young men, maidens, little children, and women. (Ezek 9:6 NASB)
>
> But these enemies of mine, who did not want me to reign over them, bring them here and slay them in my presence. (Luke 19:27 NASB)
>
> ... and will throw them into the furnace of fire; in that place there will be weeping and gnashing of teeth. (Matt 13:42 NASB)

These are just a few examples of the numerous violent biblical passages. However, there is one essential distinction between the Bible and the Qur'an:

> The Bible is a collection of stories written by at least 40 different authors, but the Qur'an is literally the word of Allah!

Here are some examples of qur'anic texts relating to non-believers:

> Kill them wherever you come upon them and drive them out of the places from which they have driven you out. For persecution is far worse than killing. And do not fight them at the Sacred Mosque unless they attack you there. If they do so, then fight them—that is the reward of the disbelievers. (Q Al-Baqarah 2:191)
>
> The retribution of those who wage war against Allah and His Messengers and strive to create disorder in the land is only that they be killed or crucified, or that their hands and their feet one right and the other left, be cut off, or that they be expelled from the land. That will be a disgrace to them in this world, and in the Hereafter they will receive a great punishment. (Q Al-Ma'idah 5:33)

A Quick Look at Religion

> When the sacred months have passed, slay the idolaters wherever you find them and take them captive, and besiege them, and prepare for them each ambush. But if they repent and keep the prayer and pay the Zakat, then leave their way clear. Verily, Allah is forgiving, Merciful. (Q At-Tawbah 9:5)[6]

I cannot imagine that any God would call for the elimination of nonbelievers. Therefore, could not some of the qur'anic texts have come from Muhammad himself, or from third parties? Moreover, how did the archangel Gabriel *de facto* reveal himself? Did he appear physically in front of Muhammad or only in Muhammad's *mind*? In the latter case, the dividing line between fantasy and reality is thin. Let's not forget, Muhammad could neither read nor write. The archangel Gabriel whispered the qur'anic verses to him over a period of some twenty-three years; Muhammad memorized these texts and had them written down by others. And then it took another twenty years after the Prophet's death (AD 632) for the Qur'an to be completed. Is it difficult to conceive that in those decades of transmission in that oral/written tradition, inconsistencies and misinterpretations may have occurred?

If, purely hypothetically, you superimpose the history of Christianity and Islam one-to-one in time, Islam is currently in the late Middle Ages. This perhaps explains why so many Muslims adhere to the texts of the Qur'an literally, just as the Christians did during that phase of Christianity at the time. Taking the comparison further, the Enlightenment in Islam could be imminent. But again, this is a purely hypothetical thought, as there is no reason to assume that the history of the two religions should necessarily be parallel.

So, what can possibly explain this firm qur'anic belief, is the fact that paradise (Arabic: *al-djannah*, "the garden") is a source of motivation for Muslims, something they look forward to and covet. The Prophet tells that those who end up in paradise will have the chance to see Allah and that believers in paradise will be

---

6. Qur'anic passages from Jansz and Kool, *Islam*, 334.

with those they love. Paradise is described frequently and in great detail in the Qur'an. An example:

> It is sparkling light, aromatic plants, a lofty palace, a flowing river, ripe fruit, a beautiful wife and abundant clothing, in an eternal abode of radiant joy, in beautiful soundly-constructed houses. Bricks of gold and silver, and mortar of fragrant musk, pebbles of pearl and sapphire, and soil of saffron. Whoever enters it is filled with joy and will never feel miserable; he will live there forever and never die, their clothes will never wear out and their youth will never fade. Allah indeed spoke the truth when He said: "And when you look there [in paradise] you will see a delight [that cannot be imagined] and a great dominion." (Quran 76:20)[7]

But . . . paradise is only attainable if one strictly adheres to the precepts of the Qur'an. If not, eternal damnation in hellfire irrevocably awaits.

JUDAISM

Judaism has no binding religious doctrine to which every Jew agrees. However, what binds Jews is their history, rules of conduct, and traditions. According to the Jews, God (Yahweh) made a covenant with Abraham, promising him that he would become the progenitor of many nations and that his descendants would take possession of the land of Canaan. For the Jews, Moses is the most important prophet as Yahweh chose Moses to deliver the Jewish people from the grip of the Egyptians, and lead them to the promised land of Israel. Moses climbed Mount Sinai, Yahweh explained the Torah to him, and handed him the two tablets containing the Ten Commandments. According to Jewish belief, Moses wrote the Torah, the first five books of the Hebrew Bible, himself.

The main differences from Christianity are as follows:

---

7. Soleyman, *Purpose of Life*, 280; brackets in the original.

A Quick Look at Religion

- The Jews do not recognize the Trinity (Father, Son, and the Holy Spirit). According to the Jews, there is only one God, namely Yahweh.
- Jesus is considered a false prophet and/or messiah. This is also why Jews do not recognize the New Testament.
- Images of saints and angels are considered idolatry.
- The Jews expect that their messiah is yet to come.

As with Christianity and Islam, I cannot find any meaningful words about the reliability of this oral/written chain of storytelling, which in the case of the Jews extended over a period of about three to four thousand years. The creation story according to Jews, Christians, and Muslims, however, is almost parallel. This means that any discrepancies between the biblical creation story and that of natural science apply to Christians, Muslims, and Jews alike.

Faith in God has provided hope, guidance, and comfort to many people. On the other hand, religions have in the past, and continue to do so today, unleashed many wars and other atrocities. On balance, more human suffering has been caused by religious fabrications, which have stubbornly clung to our civilization since time immemorial.

3

Considering Philosophy

PHILOSOPHY IS THE SCIENCE of asking questions, questions that cannot be answered in the ordinary human world, but which the philosopher attempts to answer. However, the answer itself is debated, and the original or another philosopher then formulates an even more profound answer. This answer, too, is again questioned, and so on and so forth, and so the carousel of philosophy keeps spinning. In this sense, philosophy is a wonderful science. Those who claim the most nonsensical things can hardly ever be refuted. I am even joined in this by Ludwig Wittgenstein (1889–1951), not the least of philosophers, who stated in his Tractatus Logico Philosophicus: "Most propositions and questions, that have been written about philosophical matters, are not false, but senseless. We cannot, therefore, answer questions of this kind at all, but only state their senselessness."[1]

Where philosophy and physics meet is in the phase of hypothesis setting. These hypotheses can take the strangest forms and sometimes lead to surprisingly novel ways of thinking. However in physics, nonsensical hypotheses are rejected almost immediately, where in philosophy they remain in the books, as metaphysical statements cannot be tested.

---

1. Connelly, *Wittgenstein Early Analytic Semantics*, 83.

Considering Philosophy

An example is the body-mind problem. On the one hand, there are the monists who claim that body and mind cannot exist separately; on the other, there are the dualists who claim that body and mind are two separate entities. There are even philosophers—so-called idealists—who claim that the body doesn't exist at all; they only recognize the existence of the mind! A philosopher may find this a sensible thought, but for a no-nonsense person, this is utterly ridiculous. I'd like to hear from the idealists how they envisage human reproduction without a body.

Anyway, only one of the aforementioned currents, either monism or dualism, can be true. If we ever find out which of the two is correct, it immediately follows that the other is proven nonsensical. In other words, philosophers can keep on claiming nonsensical things as long as their statements cannot be tested.

To be clear, personally, I have no problem with philosophy as such, but philosophy itself may have problems with the way some philosophers approach philosophy. Let me cite a couple of examples:

- Philosophers often don't clearly define their concepts and principles. Many even use their own definitions of certain concepts. For instance, what one philosopher calls "mind," another calls "soul" or vice versa. As a result, they build a philosophical house on shaky foundations. They should take an example from mathematicians, who clearly formulate concepts and premises in the form of axioms.

- Philosophers regularly tangle with the rules of logic. For example, people apply *common sense* to distinguish between believers and nonbelievers regarding the existence of God. In philosophy, there are also atheists and agnostics, and within these, theistic agnostics and atheistic agnostics.

Let's examine these philosophical categories: to prove that God exists, it's enough to actually observe God once. As we saw earlier, Moses had that opportunity, only he never provided evidence for his encounter. Conclusion: no one, except perhaps Moses, can to this day claim with certainty that God exists. Atheists, by definition, do not believe in the existence of God. They forget to add here that they can never, on scientific grounds, prove that God does not exist; in fact, nobody can. Therefore, no atheist can rule out God, and thus every atheist is implicitly a nonbelieving agnostic. What remains are believing agnostics and nonbelieving agnostics. However, the addition "agnostics" is superfluous in the comparison. We are now back to square one. The common-sense man had it right: we are, scientifically speaking, all agnostics and there are only two flavors, believers and nonbelievers.

One of the best-known atheists is Friedrich Nietzsche (1844–1900); witness his statement "God is dead."[2] This is, at the least, curious because someone who claims that God is dead apparently assumes that God must have once lived. However, to me this seems to be completely at odds with Nietzsche's view. Although, with Nietzsche, you often don't know whether to take his statements literally or not.

> The proposition that God does not exist is in fact just as dogmatic as the proposition that God does exist.

That logic has frequently been misapplied by philosophers is evident, for example, by the fruitless attempts to prove the existence of God through logic, as we saw in chapter 1. Perhaps the pursuit of a desired outcome or the quest for scientific recognition got in the way of carefulness when applying the rules of logic!

Sometimes philosophers make the mistake of getting too close to the realm of natural science with their assertions. For example, the French philosopher René Descartes stated that body-mind communication would take place via the pineal gland in the brain.[3] Of course, this statement is easily tested by removing the pineal gland from a test subject and observing what happens. But even that isn't necessary, as with today's medical knowledge, it is known that as people age, the pineal gland shrivels up or stops functioning altogether. Nevertheless, in these people, body-mind traffic continues as usual. So that puts an end to Descartes's belief.

The German philosophers in particular, notably Kant, Hegel, Schopenhauer, and Nietzsche, had a habit of employing

2. Bishop, *Companion to Friedrich Nietzsche*, 177.
3. McCann, *Endocrinology*, 218.

unnecessarily complex, woolly and impenetrable reasoning. Let me take the categorical imperative of Germany's most famous philosopher, Immanuel Kant, as an example. The categorical imperative is the most important precept within Kant's practical ethics. To avoid any misunderstandings, here is the original text of the Categorical imperative as formulated by Kant in German: "Handle so, dass die Maxime deiner Handlung ein allgemeines Gesetz werden könne."[4] Freely translated, this reads, "Act in such a way that the intention [the maxim] of your action can become a general law." The next step then is to formulate the relevant intention as a generally valid law, and then check whether you can detect any logical contradiction in it. Can you still make sense of it? Applying this algorithm, incidentally, is by no means straightforward in practice. What delightfully simple then is the age-old Golden Rule of life, taken from the Bible: "Love your neighbor as yourself" (Matt 22:37–39 NIV).[5] It's not quite identical to the categorical imperative, but everyone immediately understands what is meant. But who dares criticize the great Kant? However, I note that his categorical imperative has not truly been put into practice, and seems only to be cherished by other philosophers.

Many Enlightenment philosophers practiced other branches of science besides philosophy; some examples:

- Francis Bacon (1561–1626) was a statesman, lawyer, and pioneer of the scientific method.
- René Descartes (1596–1650) was a mathematician, and inventor of the Cartesian coordinate system, but was also into optics, discovering the laws of refraction, and designing a machine to sharpen lenses.
- John Locke (1632–1704) was an economist and physician.
- Gottfried Wilhelm von Leibniz (1646–1716) was a mathematician, inventor of differential and integral calculus and the binary number system, physicist, historian, and lawyer.

---

4. Kant, *Metaphysics of Morals*, 264.
5. Leiter, *John Locke's Political Philosophy*, 213.

By this, I'm not suggesting that philosophers should become multi-scientists, but I would like to note that a thorough basic knowledge of physics can contribute to a more in-depth knowledge of metaphysics. For example, a much-debated topic in philosophy is the concept of "matter". When attempting to understand "matter" in all its essence, it's difficult to avoid quantum physics—however, there will be few philosophers who can call themselves experts in this field. So my call to philosophers is to descend from your ivory towers and get to know the wonderful world of physics!

Indeed, quantum physics has taught us that reality is quite different from what human intuition suggests. The further you penetrate into the world of the very smallest, the more mysterious that reality becomes. Here are the words of Niels Bohr, pioneer of quantum physics:

> Everything we call real is made of things that cannot be regarded as real.[6]

Unknown artist

René Descartes (1596–1650)

Apart from what I have written above, we must not forget that philosophy has sometimes had a great impact on social life

6. Tegmark, *Our Mathematical Universe.*

throughout history. However, the last serious upheaval brought about by philosophy dates back almost four centuries. It was the French philosopher René Descartes whose ideas sparked the Enlightenment in the seventeenth century. In his disputes with the scholastics—the ruling church intelligentsia—he grew to dislike the fact that they always involved God as an explanation in their arguments. Descartes wanted to do away with the dogmas of the time, church dogmas in particular. Therefore, he intended to rebuild the house of knowledge from the ground up, purely based on reason.

On a long, cold winter night in 1640, Descartes, sitting all alone in his Leiden home in the Netherlands, put quill to paper and formulated the purpose of a long-intended project: "At last I will apply myself sincerely and unreservedly to the general demolition of all of my opinions."[7] In his *Discourse on Method*, published three years earlier, he had already figured out how he would go about it: "But because I then desired to devote myself exclusively to the search for the truth, I thought it necessary . . . that I reject as absolutely false everything in which I could imagine the least doubt, in order to see whether, after this process, something in my beliefs remained that was entirely indubitable."[8] So he was looking for a true understanding of what absolute knowledge represents. In other words, he wanted to know what he could know for certain, that about which there could be no doubt.

He began by doubting his own senses. From the fact that we dream and hallucinate, Descartes drew the conclusion that our senses are not always reliable. Our perception is not infallible; perhaps we do not always experience the real, true world. If the authenticity of our experience could occasionally be questioned, that was enough for Descartes to dismiss it as absolutely false. That our senses can sometimes mislead us without our knowing, it suggests that they can mislead us all the time. And if we cannot trust information obtained through our senses, how can we confirm the existence of an external world? Perhaps nothing physical exists at

---

7. Descartes, *Discourse on Method*, 59.
8. Descartes, *Discourse on Method*, 18.

all, no sky, no earth, no bodies, and this is all an illusion, a fabrication. This led him to even doubt the mathematics he was working on because he thought that perhaps God allowed him to make mistakes, and his premises therefore might be wrong. But he could not actually believe that an all-goodness God was leading him astray. That's why he supposed that there was an extremely powerful and clever "evil genius" determined to deceive him all the time about the true nature of reality. At one point, Descartes could no longer think of anything else from which he could derive certainty. At last, he had to admit that there was nothing that could not be doubted. Here are his own words: "But eventually I am forced to admit that there is nothing among the things I once believed to be true which is not permissible to doubt—and not out of frivolity or lack of thought, but for valid and considered reasons."[9]

In effect, he had dismissed all his thoughts from being reliable. As a result, he doubted everything. However, the only thing he could not doubt was the fact that he did doubt. This he was completely sure of, and therefore there had to be an "I" that doubted, witness his statement: "That we cannot doubt of our existence while we doubt, and that is the first knowledge we acquire when we philosophize in order."[10]

"I doubt, therefore I am" was Descartes's logical conclusion at the end of his process of "methodic doubt", as the starting point for the foundation of the house of knowledge. But instead, for some unclear reason, he went one step further, and stated, "I think, therefore I am." The explanation for this little bridge can be found in his posthumously published essay *The Search for Truth through Natural Light*: "That it is necessary to know what doubt is, and what thought is, before we can be fully persuaded of this reasoning—I doubt, therefore I am—or what is the same—I think, therefore I am."[11]

We already saw that Descartes, during his process of "methodic doubt" could not for 100 percent be certain about the

---

9. Descartes, *Discourse on Method*, 62.
10. Descartes, *Principles of Philosophy*, 14 (part 1, article VII).
11. Hallam, *Introduction to the Literature*, 99.

correctness of his every thought, except for the thought "I doubt, therefore I am." It follows that he should not have equated "I doubt, therefore I am" with "I think, therefore I am," however trivial it may seem. Descartes thus went one bridge too far, and should have stuck with "I doubt, therefore I am"; even better, "I doubt, therefore I exist"; or in Latin *dubito, ergo existo*. With the first knowledge " I doubt, therefore I am" Descartes demonstrated human existence. Any other statement, including *cogito, ergo sum* adds nothing to it. Descartes's proposition—the *Cogito* is the first knowledge—is false.

From the certainty that man exists, Descartes reasons in his *Meditations* that God must also exist, and then, from the contemplation of the true God . . . to arrive at the knowledge of reality. And this completes the circle for Descartes.

The Danish philosopher Søren Kierkegaard (1813–1855) made a short shrift of "I think, therefore I am." In his *Concluding Unscientific Postscript* he rightfully remarked that the *Cogito* presupposes one's existence but does not prove it. In other words, the existence is implicit in "I think," making the addition "therefore I am" superfluous. Thinking does not prove existence, it's the other way around, existence is an indispensable condition (*conditio sine qua non*) for thinking, at least for human beings. In fact, Descartes does not say much other than "a thinking thing thinks," which led Kierkegaard to conclude: "If the 'I' which is the subject of 'cogito' means an individual human being, the proposition means nothing . . . There is no conclusion here, for the proposition is a tautology."[12]

But neither did Descartes's proofs of God hold up, as they *a priori* assumed a metaphysical presupposition. This warrants the following conclusion:

> Descartes's arguments that sparked the Enlightenment were built upon quicksand.

12. Kierkegaard, *Concluding Unscientific Postscript*, 281.

4

And Then There Was Life

THE HISTORY OF THE universe covers a period of almost fourteen billion years—such an astronomically large number we can hardly perceive it. As we are going to discuss the origin and evolution of the universe, it makes sense to reduce this immensely long period to human proportions. To do so, we'll use the so-called cosmic calendar. This works as follows: the period of about fourteen billion years is projected onto one calendar year. On 1 January at 00:00, the beginning of the cosmic calendar, the big bang took place, and at the end of the cosmic calendar, 31 December at 24:00, we have reached "now," as we speak. The cosmic calendar is therefore a rolling calendar.

Example: the dinosaurs died out sixty-six million years ago due to the impact of an asteroid in Mexico, after having dominated planet earth for two hundred million years.[1] On the cosmic calendar, this represents a surprisingly recent date, namely 30 December. We note this cosmic date as [30 December] so as not to confuse it with a real date.

> On the cosmic calendar, an average human life lasts less than one second!

1. "Chicxulub."

And Then There Was Life

On 1 January at 00:00, humans usher in the New Year. On our cosmic calendar, the big bang also took place on [1 January at 00:00]. I would advocate renaming New Year's Day as Big Bang Day. To celebrate the start of the new year, impressive fireworks are set off around 00:00 in many places in the world. Isn't it amazingly appropriate? This is the time to remember that humans are made of stardust and that we're nothing at all in the immense universe, like ants in the Sahara desert. Perhaps it's not a bad idea to start every new year with a contemplation in humility.

THE BIG BANG [1 JANUARY 00:00]

In the beginning, there was the big bang. This took place 13.8 billion years ago,[2] in an infinitely small space with an infinitely large mass density, the so-called big bang singularity. Renowned cosmologist Lawrence Krauss goes one step further and is convinced that the universe was created out of nothing (*ex nihilo*).[3] Purely coincidentally, *creatio ex nihilo* is also a Christian dogma (2 Macc 7:28). Immediately in the very first second of the big bang, the temperature jumped to gigantic values and the universe began to expand exponentially from an area way smaller than a proton to an area about the size of a meter in a tiny fraction of a second.[4] After this inflationary outburst, the expansion continued but was countered by gravitational forces. In images, the big bang is often represented as an explosion into empty space. This depiction is incorrect. In the first place, there was no light at that time, because no stars existed yet. Second, there was no bang, because no medium in which sound could propagate existed yet. Nor was there an "explosion" into empty space, for empty space was created precisely by the big bang. The big bang was a silent, dark, inflationary hyperexpansion into nothingness.

2. "Age of the Universe."
3. Krauss, *Universe from Nothing*.
4. Guth and Kaiser, "Inflationary Cosmology."

We now know that the atomic nuclei of the light elements, particularly hydrogen, helium, and lithium, were formed ten to six hundred seconds after the big bang[5]. It took 380,000 years for the universe to cool down enough for electrons, which had hitherto roamed freely, to start binding to protons and neutrons, forming the first atoms[6].

Then, concentrations of hydrogen and helium molecules created gas clouds in various places in the universe. Over time, these gas clouds grew bigger and heavier. Eventually, they imploded under their own weight, raising the temperature to a level where a nuclear fusion process was initiated. This is how the first stars were born, one hundred million years after the big bang [3 January].[7] Hydrogen is converted into helium and the resulting energy is emitted in the form of heat and light. The heavier elements such as carbon, oxygen, and iron are formed through nuclear fusion in the interior of stars. Eventually, these elements are spit out into space by exploding stars at the end of their lifetime. Hence, humans are not made of big bang dust, but *stardust*. In fact, almost all of the stuff around us was formed in the heart of stars!

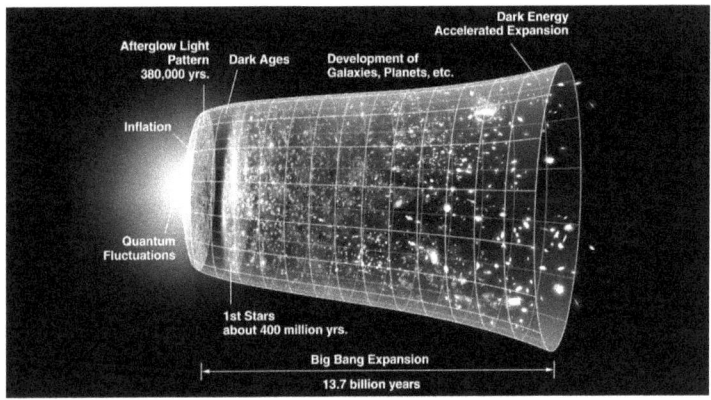

NASA/WMAP Science Team, 2006
Figure 3. The evolution of the universe based on the big bang theory.

5. "Big Bang Nucleosynthesis."
6. "The Early Universe."
7. "Potential First Traces."

And Then There Was Life

Our sun formed about 4.6 billion years ago [2 September] from a cloud of rotating gas.[8] Planets, like the earth, generally form as flat, rotating disks of dust and gas around young stars. Matter then starts to stick together and the resulting clump, as it gets bigger, binds more and more matter to itself. This is how our earth came into being [2 September] at the same time as our solar system.

An exception to the formation process of a planet is the moon, the only planet that orbits the earth. The moon was originated when the earth collided with a small planet, the size of Mars, at the time of the formation of our solar system. From the resulting debris, matter then clumped together forming the moon, about 60–175 million years after the birth of the solar system [3–7 September].[9]

The development of the big bang theory was possible thanks to Einstein's theory of relativity and insights into quantum physics. As early as 1948, physicists predicted that radiation from the extremely hot phase of the very early universe should still be present. This so-called "cosmic microwave background radiation" was first measured in 1965 in an experiment conducted by Americans Penzias and Wilson, providing the best evidence that the big bang actually took place.

Curiously, in the early years of television, anyone could witness the cosmic background radiation on their own analog TV. As soon as broadcasting stopped at the end of the evening, a vibrating grey image with white noise appeared on the tube. To some extent, this "snow" was caused by microwave radiation coming from this very hot phase of the big bang. So if there was nothing on TV, you could still watch the birth of the universe.

In the theory of the cosmos, you regularly come across the prefix "dark," for example in "dark matter" and "dark energy." Physicists use these prefixes to indicate that not all the physical secrets of the phenomenon in question have (yet) been unraveled. Physicists know that there must be more mass in the universe to

---

8. Choi, "Earth's Sun."
9. Warren, "How the Earth and Moon."

hold the galaxies together than we can observe, but so far this "dark matter" has not yet been detected—even with today's space telescopes. On the other hand, physicists know that the expanding force of the universe has to come from somewhere else and, for now, this is called "dark energy." It is estimated that the universe consists of 68 percent "dark energy," 27 percent "dark matter," and only 5 percent visible matter.[10] If it ever gets to the point where the general theory of relativity and quantum physics are integrated into one single theory, then the above-mentioned "dark" mysteries might be unraveled.

If the nucleus of the hydrogen atom, the proton, were the size of a golf ball, the electron would be about 3 kilometers away, on average.[11] A minuscule particle filling a huge space, that is, the space between the nucleus of the atom and the electron orbits. Of the visible matter in the universe, more than 99.999999 percent is empty space. But . . . this so-called "empty space" is never really empty. Due to random quantum fluctuations, pairs of virtual particles and antiparticles constantly arise and disappear, in accordance with Einstein's formula $E = mc^2$.

Incidentally, the term "big bang" was coined around 1950 by one of the theory's opponents, British astronomer Fred Hoyle (1915–2001). He assumed, just like Einstein, that the universe was a static entity without beginning or end, the so-called "steady state theory." Since then, the term "big bang" has stuck.

EMERGENCE AND DEVELOPMENT OF LIFE

For the first five hundred million years of the earth's existence, the temperature was so high that no life was possible. Over time, the earth cooled down to the point where water vapor was able to condense and it started raining; this continued for millions of years. As a result, the oceans formed, covering almost the entire earth's surface—which, at the same time, was continually ravaged

---

10. Shaver, *Rise of Science*, 52.
11. Ford, *Quantum World*, 10–11.

by earthquakes, volcanic eruptions, asteroids and comet impacts as well as by ultraviolet radiation from the sun. Under these harsh conditions, about 4.1 billion years ago [14 September], the first primitive cells[12] arose from organic chemicals floating around in the warm "primordial soup." These were bacteria which supplied oxygen to the atmosphere through photosynthesis. Charles Darwin was the first to assume that these single-celled organisms were the origin of all life on earth, the so-called *last universal common ancestor* (LUCA).

Initially, organic molecules such as amino acids were formed from inorganic substances. In 1953 Americans Stanley Miller and Harold Urey confirmed this experimentally by showing that complex amino acids—the building blocks of proteins—could arise spontaneously.[13] Here we have arrived at the stage where an evolutionary process took place, in which a primitive form of life emerged from simple organic compounds. This phenomenon, called abiogenesis, is now widely accepted scientifically, although not all the details are yet known.

Originally it was thought that the first self-replicating molecules were based on RNA (a primitive form of DNA) and that the DNA molecule would have emerged from it later on. However, in 2020, chemists working at the Scripps Research Institute in San Diego California discovered that DNA and RNA could arise simultaneously and that the first self-replicating molecules—the first forms of life on earth—were a hybrid of the two.[14]

We've now arrived at the point where these first simple cells developed into more complex cells—named "eukaryotes" about two billion years ago [9 November]. Eukaryotes have a nucleus in which the hereditary information is stored, and so-called organelles—the cell's "mini-organs," often surrounded by a membrane, which have a particular function, for example, energy supply, breakdown of waste products, or metabolism of proteins.

From these, three groups of living organisms developed:

12. "Earliest Known Life Forms."
13. Akre and Rafferty, "Miller-Urey Experiment."
14. "Discovery Boosts Theory."

- fungi such as mushrooms and lichens [6 December],
- primitive animals such as sponges, arthropods, and jellyfish [16 December],
- plants [19 December] and then trees [21 December].

The first fish swam in the oceans around 500 million years ago [17 December] and they continued to evolve in the water until about 360 million years ago [22 December]. The fins of some of these fish developed into a kind of legs, allowing them to crawl across the seabed, and soon after they crawled onto land as amphibians.

Zina Deretsky, 2009
Figure 4. Fish go ashore for the first time.

These amphibians then transformed into reptiles and from these—about 200 million years ago [26 December]—evolved the first mammals. The platypus and the echidna are the only two survivors from an early branching lineage within mammals. Much later—12.3 million years ago [31 December 14:24], an ape species, the hominids, emerged consisting of humans, chimpanzees, gorillas, and orangutans.

It is a widespread misconception that humans descended from chimpanzees; however, humans are closest to the chimpanzee

And Then There Was Life

in terms of gene structure. DNA research from the University of Washington has shown how much humans differ from chimps: "While there has only been a 1 per cent change in the shared genes of chimps and humans in 6 million years, each species has also either added or dropped 1.5 per cent of their genes."[15] This means that currently, humans and chimps are genetically 96 percent similar!

Homo sapiens (thinking man) is thought to have appeared in Africa about 300,000 years ago [31 December at 23:48].[16] Recent excavations by researchers from the Max Planck Institute for Evolutionary Anthropology in Leipzig have found fossilized skull remains near Marrakesh, Morocco dated at around 280,000 to 350,000 years ago.[17] From Africa, *Homo sapiens* spread across the rest of the world. In Europe, these first humans encountered the Neanderthals, but this species later became extinct. *The rest is history.*

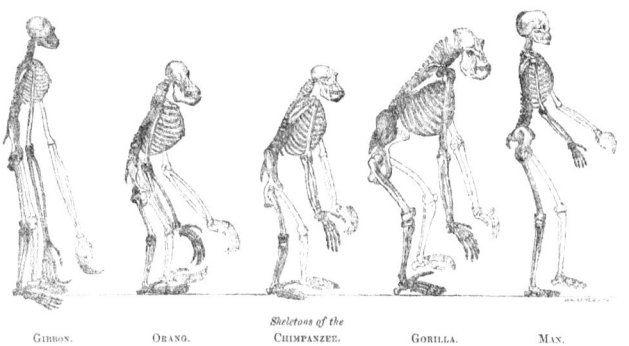

Waterhouse Hawkins, 1863

Figure 5. Drawing from the book *Evidence as to Man's Place in Nature* by English biologist Thomas Henry Huxley (1825–1895) in which he set out to demonstrate the kinship between apes and humans. An ardent supporter of the theory of evolution, he was nicknamed *Darwin's Bulldog*.

---

15. Scotney, *Theory of Evolution*, 159.
16. "Homo Sapiens."
17. Wong, "Oldest Homo Sapiens," 12.

5

The Accidental Universe

WHAT HAPPENED BEFORE THE big bang?
This is as interesting a question as it is nonsensical. At the moment of the big bang, the universe was concentrated in an infinitely small space with an infinitely large mass density, the big bang singularity. After that, everything came into existence. Please note: this includes not only matter and energy but also empty space, and even time. The clock started ticking. Before the big bang, there was no time!
So, how do we know this?
In 1965, an important event took place in physics. British mathematician and physicist Roger Penrose (1931–present) showed, under the assumption that the general theory of relativity is correct, that a star collapsing due to gravity has to end in a singularity. For this proof, Penrose received the Nobel Prize. This singularity has since been renamed a "black hole." Figure 23 in the Einstein appendix shows a graphic representation of a black hole. The only twenty-four-year-old Stephen Hawking then applied Penrose's mathematical model in the opposite direction to the entire universe and showed that an expanding universe must have started with a singularity: the big bang singularity. In a singularity, the curvature of space-time is infinite (see appendix 3: "Albert Einstein"), the laws of nature lose their validity, and space and time

lose their meaning. Therefore, you cannot talk about a time before the big bang, because it simply didn't exist. Nor can you talk about a temperature lower than zero degrees Kelvin (minus 273 degrees Celsius), because at zero degrees Kelvin all atoms are stationary. So similarly, lower than absolute zero simply doesn't exist. As prior to the big bang, there was no time, no God could have existed to create the universe.

In chapter 4, we saw that

1. life emerged spontaneously out of non-living material (abiogenesis);
2. the first multicellular organisms arose, through cell division based on RNA and DNA, out of single-cellular organisms;
3. these multicellular organisms evolved, via a long pathway, into mammals, amongst others; and
4. humans evolved from a specific species of apes.

This chain of events is fully explainable by Charles Darwin's theory of evolution (see appendix 2).

Now we can see that the discrepancy between the biblical creation story and the version according to natural science regarding the creation of man is beginning to take on extreme proportions. According to the Bible, God created man on the sixth day. According to physics, it took almost ten billion years before conditions on earth were at all suitable for the emergence of life. Only then could the first primitive life forms develop through abiogenesis, but not by his hand. Furthermore, it took a complex evolutionary chain of about four billion years to convert single-celled organisms into *Homo sapiens*. All this time, God was glaringly absent.

> Only when everything was already there, God came to bring a few stone tables to instruct the evolved ape on how to behave.

We haven't yet encountered any discontinuities or gaps in the evolution of man and the universe where any possible intervention by God could be assumed. In other words, there is no "God of the gaps." The evolution of both man and the universe is completely explainable from natural science. Hence I arrive at the following conclusion:

> The evolution of man and the universe was an autonomous process and God played no role in it.

One might wonder what triggered the big bang when time started ticking. Stephen Hawking (1942–2018) says that when you look at matter at the subatomic level, "you enter a world where conjuring something out of nothing is indeed possible. At least, very briefly. That's because at this scale particles, like protons, behave according to the laws of nature we call quantum physics. And they really can arise randomly, hang around for a while, and then disappear, only to reappear somewhere else. Since we know that the universe itself was once very small, smaller than a proton, this is remarkable; it means that the universe itself, in all its mind-boggling vastness and complexity, could have originated with a bang without violating the laws of nature. . . . The laws of nature itself tell us that not only could the universe have popped into existence without any assistance, like a proton, and have required nothing in terms of energy, but also that it is possible that nothing caused the Big Bang. Nothing."[1]

Here, Hawking refers to random quantum fluctuations during the big bang. These fluctuations caused tiny variations in the uniform density of the primordial universe, which were magnified during the ultra-short outburst of hyperinflation. In regions with higher densities, expansion slowed down due to gravitational forces. Eventually, these regions could implode under their own weight, and form galaxies and stars.

It is obvious that without these random quantum fluctuations, no galaxies and stars would have formed, and hence man would not have existed either. Incidentally, chance plays a similar role in evolutionary processes because each new generation of organisms starts off with genetic material in which random changes (mutations) have occurred (see appendix 2: "Charles Darwin"). Without these mutations, evolution would not work.

1. Hawking, *Brief Answers*, 33–35.

The Accidental Universe

In order to understand the behavior of the very smallest particles, we have to make a giant leap from the ordinary human world to the world of quantum physics. Among physicists, this is a widely accepted theory about the behavior of the very smallest particles; particles smaller than atoms and even smaller than protons or neutrons. Albert Einstein pioneered quantum physics in 1905 by launching the idea that light propagates as indivisible packets (quanta) of energy, later known as "photons." Quantum physics is an extremely complex field, and it seems to be completely at odds with human intuition. Nevertheless, in appendix 4, I have attempted to shed at least a little light on this strange but valid theory.

One might also wonder where the laws of nature come from. After twenty years of research, Stephen Hawking and the Belgian cosmologist Thomas Hertog (1975–present) arrived at the revolutionary insight that the big bang is not only the beginning of time, but that the laws of nature were not preset, and evolved alongside the universe coming into being: "Our top-down perspective reverses the hierarchy between laws and reality in physics. It leads to a new philosophy of physics that rejects the idea that the universe is a machine governed by unconditional laws and replaces it with the view that the universe is a kind of self-organizing entity, in which all sorts of emergent patterns appear, the most general of which we call the laws of physics."[2] However, their theory has yet to be put to the test.

The fairy tale of Adam and Eve has long since been debunked, however those who argue that we should take a symbolic view of the biblical creation story will also have to think again. God was not involved whatsoever in the creation of man and the universe. The entire biblical creation story can therefore be scrapped.

| The book of Genesis can be deleted from the Bible!

This statement, of course, is significant: the Torah, of which the book of Genesis is a part, is considered by Jews to be the most important book in the Hebrew Bible. Moreover, Moses, the Jews's

---

2. Hertog, *On the Origin of Time*, 258.

most important prophet, is said to have written the book of Genesis himself—even though theologians are hotly debating whether Moses wrote the Torah completely by himself. Slowly but surely, natural science is undermining the story of God's true influence on mankind.

6

The Ascension of the Spirit

As an interlude, let's conduct a thought experiment on what happens—subject to the prevailing laws of nature—to believers in God when they take their last breath. Obviously, all objects formed after the big bang, such as stars and planets, are subject to the laws of nature that govern our universe. The same applies to man, that is, both in body and mind. Let this sink in:

| Humans are 100 percent stardust!

Everyone will agree that a human body, buried after death, will decay slowly. This process can, of course, be accelerated by cremation, but the result remains the same. The body is the easy part. In the Abrahamic religions, it is assumed that the incorporeal part of man goes to the afterlife after death. But what is this incorporeal part of man and where is the afterlife? Above all, let's not get into a discussion here about the differences between the spirit, the soul, the mind, or otherwise, but, from now on, let's—completely arbitrarily—refer to "the spirit" as the incorporeal part of man that goes to the afterlife. The other question is where is the afterlife? It seems implausible that the afterlife is somewhere within our own universe as we shall see later—our universe is not infinite in time—and that's inconsistent with the idea of an eternal God in an eternal God's house. Let's therefore assume that the afterlife is somewhere outside our universe in a parallel universe, where perhaps completely different laws of nature apply.

The Journey of the Spirit to the Afterlife

Obviously, wherever the afterlife is, the spirit must first leave our universe (I'm not addressing here the hypothetical idea that there might be a shortcut between different universes, commonly referred to by the term "wormhole"). According to the Abrahamic religions, after death, the spirit goes to the afterlife in a timeless movement, but science does not get away with that. The body, as well as the spirit, is made of stardust and is as such subject to the laws of nature that govern our universe. As the spirit supposedly has no mass, it can travel to the afterlife at up to the speed of light (300,000 km/second). For the sake of convenience, we'll not even think about how the spirit can get to this speed! Along the way, the spirit encounters all sorts of dangers—for example, black holes. I'm not sure whether God could even escape from a black hole—after all, God comes from another universe with perhaps different laws of nature—but the spirit certainly cannot. Once the spirit is sucked into one of the billions of black holes, it would *never ever* be able to reach the afterlife; nothing can escape from a black hole!

Furthermore, I suspect that the spirit had better not get too close to the scorching heat of the stars, temperatures up to 200,000 Kelvin[1]—temperatures you might consider "hell-like"! Moreover, the spirit must avoid collisions with planets and asteroids in the two trillion[2] galaxies within our universe. Therefore, the spirit should have access to an excellent *universal positioning system*. The distance from the earth to the *observable* edge of our universe is about forty-six billion light years.[3] In other words, it will take the spirit at least forty-six billion years to get there. But the spirit will have to travel much longer than this, because our universe keeps

1. Battersby, "Eight Extremes."
2. Castelvecchi, "Universe."
3. Betz, "Where Is the Edge."

on expanding. Then, the spirit still has to bridge the undoubtedly gigantic distance between the observable edge and the *actual* edge of our universe, if the latter exists at all.[4] From there, it will have to continue its journey to God's universe. We now have reached the point where we can no longer use our imagination, because outside our universe other laws of nature may apply. Obviously, if the spirit cannot reach the afterlife, this applies unquestionably to the inert body—according to Islam, the body also goes to paradise! Considering all of the above, the following conclusion seems justified:

> It is extremely unlikely that the spirit can ever reach the afterlife. Man is trapped within the universe.

This thought experiment may sound ridiculous, but it's not my intention to make fun of people's beliefs. It's merely a logical deduction based on the premises I formulated. An imaginary solution for the dying person might be to send the following signal to the afterlife: *Beam me up, God.*

---

4. Baird, "Where Is the Edge."

7

The Body-Spirit Issue

IN THE PREVIOUS CHAPTER, we implicitly assumed that the spirit detaches from the body after death and ascends to the afterlife, but is that really what happens? For as long as philosophy has existed, the body-spirit problem has been a recurring theme. Basically, there are two opposing currents in philosophy: monism and dualism. Monists state that the body and mind are one indivisible entity, whereas dualists believe that the body and mind are two separate substances. However, which of the two currents is the true one, philosophers are happy to leave it to their readers. Let us first become acquainted with the views of some well-known philosophers on this controversial issue.

The Body-Spirit Issue

Unknown artist

Plato (427–347 BC)

Plato saw matter, including the human body, as something impermanent and therefore inferior. However, he regarded the soul as eternal and superior. According to him, the soul was actually trapped in the body and should be freed, so that only then could it arrive at pure truth. Plato was thus a dualist. Incidentally, a few centuries later, his position was adopted in its entirety by the Roman Catholic Church.

God Yes? God No?

After Lysippos, 390–300 BC

Aristotle (348–322 BC)

For Aristotle, the soul, as part of the body, is mortal. In this respect, Aristotle's doctrine would clash with Christianity, where the soul, while connected to the body, can exist independently. Aristotle was therefore a monist. Later, the Roman Catholic Church also distinguished between the spirit and the soul. The spirit represents intuition, conscience, and God-consciousness, while the soul stands for feeling, wanting, and thinking. The spirit returns to God and the soul goes to the realm of the dead.

The Body-Spirit Issue

John Michael Wright, 1617–1694

Thomas Hobbes (1588–1679)

According to Thomas Hobbes, there was only one physical world, namely the world of matter. He denied the existence of an immaterial reality. Immaterial substance, according to him, was nonsense. The existence of consciousness was an illusion. Hobbes was clearly a radical monist.

After Frans Hals, 1649–1700

René Descartes (1596–1650)

Descartes increasingly disliked arguing with scholastics as they always included God in their reasoning. With *cogito, ergo sum*, Descartes started building his thinking from scratch and distanced himself from the scholasticism of the Middle Ages. This heralded the Age of Enlightenment, in which reason became the main guide of thought. It remains curious that Descartes, the enlightened thinker *par excellence*, did not distance himself from dualism, one of the basic values of scholasticism.

The Current State of Play

In the second half of the twentieth century, monism has increasingly pushed dualism into the background. Nowadays, few philosophers defend a variant of dualism. Interestingly the Bible says, "For you are dust, And to dust you shall return" (Gen 3:19 NASB), a truism.

The Body-Spirit Issue

Unknown photographer, 1911

Duncan MacDougall (1866–1920)

US doctor Duncan MacDougall conducted the following medical experiment. He weighed patients immediately before and after death. He found that they weighed twenty-one grams less on average after death, thus coming to the hilarious conclusion that these twenty-one grams had to belong to the soul that had left the body. Needless to say, this experiment had no scientific value whatsoever.

Again: The Ascension of the Spirit

In the previous chapter on the ascension of the spirit, I concluded that, practically spoken, the spirit, consisting of stardust, is not likely at all to reach the boundaries of the universe, let alone the afterlife. However, if we assume the monistic view that with death both body and the spirit die, a problem arises for those who believe in God. How will they get "there" now that the spirit also dies?

But another complication arises, and it is this: What about the ascension of those suffering from irreversible brain damage, such as dementia? Will they suffer eternal dementia in the afterlife? Or what about people with psychiatric disorders who are in a permanent depression? Will they stay in that forever? But I worry most about Stephen Hawking, whose speech computer is still somewhere in Cambridge. It must be a terrible torment for him not to be able to communicate with God and Einstein in the afterlife.

Yet, even the immortality of persons without physical or mental illnesses raises questions. Take as an example a young boy, who dies at the age of ten because of a traffic accident. Does this boy remain in heaven at this level of intellect forever? Or is his mind upgraded to grown-up status? Now suppose that this boy would have reached the grown-up status at the age of say thirty, then he would be missing his own personal development over a twenty-year period. But also, his personality would partly have been shaped by accidental events, which cannot be reconstructed afterwards. This means that the aforementioned artificial intervention creates a totally different personality from that of the person had the accident not happened. Therefore, such an intervention by God does not seem right. On the other hand, it also does not seem right that such a boy should remain in child status for all eternity. Immortality is apparently a barrel full of contradictions and question marks.

According to Christian doctrine, we need not worry about these issues. God solves them because he is all-powerful, all-knowing, and all-good ("all" in the sense of "perfect"). However, these attributes are mutually contradictory.

An example: in his all-knowledge, God should have seen coming what Putin was planning to do. In his all-goodness, he should have prevented the consequences of Putin's actions by, in his all-powerfulness, ensuring that he had a fatal fall from his horse. Or less crudely, he could have ensured that Putin's father had become infertile, at least before Vladimir's conception. But God did nothing at all. Besides, an omnipotent God, strictly speaking,

The Body-Spirit Issue

contradicts himself because he cannot, for example, make a stone that he himself cannot lift. Furthermore, God apparently did not see fit to reveal himself to mankind again after meeting Moses. God seemingly has chosen not to intervene at all, and is just watching the show. Perhaps somewhere in his bubble, he's enjoying watching humanity destroy itself.

But let me stop speculating here because God's ways are inscrutable—"and rarely pleasant"—as one of my Protestant friends usually adds.

8

Answering the Big Questions

IN CHAPTER 5, I arrived at the conclusion that a possible creator did not (yet) interfere with our universe. Perhaps, with the accidental universe in mind, it might be possible to say something more about the big questions arising from past philosophers. It would be extremely interesting, but unfortunately only imaginary, if these philosophers could consider the core questions of philosophy with present-day knowledge. For now, therefore, you'll have to make do with what I've imagined! Let's review some of these questions.

WHAT IS MANKIND?

Several philosophers have answered this question over time, in particular naming our distinction from animals. The Greek philosopher Aristotle described man as an *animal rationale*, or reasonable animal. Reason is thus the characteristic that distinguishes humans from animals. According to the cultural philosopher Max Scheler, the most important characteristics of humans are feelings and love. And the atheist Jean-Paul Sartre stated that it is our freedom to determine our own destiny. Sigmund Freud assumes that humans, as descendants of animals, are still subconsciously driven by instinct and passion.

Answering the Big Questions

Man is probably the most intelligent creature of all living organisms in a place in the universe where the physical conditions (water, oxygen, CO_2, temperature, et cetera) were so favorable that spontaneous development of life took place. It may seem as if planet earth was made for us, as if there was a preconceived plan, but that is only a pretense. If the cosmic parameters on earth had been even a fraction different to what they are now, mankind simply would not have existed, at least not on this planet. All this has to do with the tuning of the constants of nature, the fixed values in physical formulas. Consider, for example, the speed of light "c," the gravitational constant "G," or Planck's constant "h." Cosmologists have discovered that if these values deviate even a fraction from the current values, atoms, stars and planets cannot exist. Obviously, (human) life would then be unthinkable. This phenomenon is referred to as the fine-tuning argument. Theists and other creationists seize on the fine-tuning argument as evidence for the existence of God and an intelligent designer, respectively. Although the burden of proof of an assertion rests in principle with the person making the assertion, creationists do not as yet yield. Apparently, creationists rather believe than try to prove things. Anyway, the fact that some mystery has not yet been resolved can, of course, never count as evidence.

Creationists assume that a creator set the constants of nature *a priori*. One wonders when that might have been. It is obvious that it must have taken place before the big bang. As we saw earlier, time only started ticking at $t = 0$ of the big bang, so one cannot speak of time before the big bang. Therefore, the question when fine-tuning by a creator actually took place remains unanswered.

A common explanation for the fine-tuning argument from the camp of naturalists (the opponents of creationists) has its origins in quantum physics. In the second half of the last century, physicists concluded that the multiverse is an inescapable, logical consequence of cosmic inflation or string theory. The multiverse is seized upon by naturalists to explain the bio-friendly nature of planet earth in simple terms. The reasoning is as follows: if many, if not infinitely many universes exist, then there is a real chance that there is at least one universe, like ours, whose constants of nature are set in such a way that a spontaneous form of life can arise. To this day, however, the existence of the multiverse has not been confirmed empirically, because observations in the multiverse are only imaginary. In case you have read chapter 6, "The Ascension of the Spirit," you'll understand that, practically spoken, anything, even traveling near the speed of light cannot go beyond our universe.

One can further wonder whether the values of the constants of nature are set in stone. Several physicists, and not the least, Paul Dirac, Victor Stenger, and Paul Davies, to name a few, believe that constants of nature are time dependent. Their reasoning is that they formed during the inflationary period of the big bang, and underwent a major change in that fraction of a second. As the universe continued to cool down over billions of years, these constants of nature seemed unchanging, but they were in fact still subject to minuscule changes. It is expected that in future, with more precise measurement methods, this issue can be resolved empirically. If it turns out that one or more (fundamental) constants of nature are actually time dependent, and a creator therefore has not fixed these values *a priori*, the fine-tuning argument is no longer valid.

But again, the earth was not made for mankind, it's the other way around: man is an accidental inhabitant of a planet where life was possible. Doesn't our universe, consisting of two trillion galaxies, lead us to consider that similar conditions may occur elsewhere? Here is the answer from the renowned American physicist Victor J. Stenger (1935–2014): "Any huge, random universe, regardless of its properties, will naturally develop at least a few tiny pockets of complexity within a vast sea of chaos, which is just what we seem to see in our universe. We do not need either a designer or multiple universes to account for such rare deviations as are consistent with chance."[1]

Although both physics and evolutionary theory fall under the realm of natural science, there is a crucial difference between the two. The latter is based on random variations (mutations) in genetic material. It is therefore only possible to describe and explain

---

1. Stenger, *God: The Failed Hypothesis*, 163.

the evolutionary process in retrospect. This contrasts with physics, which has a predictive character. If the evolutionary process could be repeated, by no means certain would it be that mankind would reappear on the scene. This justifies the following statement:

| Mankind is a fluke in the cosmos.

Since the Middle Ages, thanks to Copernicus, we have known that the earth is not the center of the universe. Isn't it about time we realized that also man himself is nothing special at all? Many authors on religion versus science still put man first as a unique being, chosen to inhabit the universe. But also in general, people think of themselves as elevated above everything else in the universe. Even if God existed, man is at best an accidental test result from God's experimental lab, but not God's chosen one.

Is mankind the only being in the universe? According to the book of Genesis, God made man and even created him in his image and likeness. He never mentioned that he also created other human-like creatures. Cosmically, man should have enough living space within our solar system; only then the stars would be missing from the firmament. Therefore, let's say that our galaxy with one hundred billion[2] stars should provide more than enough space. But then, why on earth did God create all the other two trillion galaxies in our universe? Surely it's therefore inconceivable to claim that our universe was created specifically for mankind.

In November 2021, the Pentagon officially announced that it would seriously investigate extraterrestrial life. The US military has formed a committee to detect and identify UFOs in US military airspace. The term "UFOs" is actually incorrect in this context. NASA itself speaks of "unidentified aerial phenomena" or "UAPs."

WHERE DO WE COME FROM?

The fact that our universe originated from the big bang is now widely accepted. Most people also generally agree that Darwin's

---

2. "Milky Way Galaxy."

theory of evolution is a plausible explanation for the development of life. In any case, no contra-evidence to the theory of evolution has been produced. Of the millions of animal fossils that have been found, there is not one that does not fit within the evolutionary time sequence.

With today's knowledge, we can note the following:

1. everything in the universe, including body and brain of humans, is made of stardust; we humans are therefore a piece of nuclear waste;
2. life emerged spontaneously out of nonliving material (abiogenesis);
3. multicellular life on earth evolved from single-cellular organisms; and
4. these multicellular organisms evolved, via a long pathway, into *Homo sapiens*, following Charles Darwin's theory of evolution.

| God did not create man, man is an evolved bacterium.

WHAT IS MANKIND'S PLACE IN THE COSMOS?

The British priest-philosopher William Paley (1743–1805), a contemporary of Charles Darwin, compared the cosmos to a mechanical watch. Just as a watch cannot arise by itself and requires a watchmaker, Paley concluded that the cosmos must also have had a creator. The watchmaker analogy is the forerunner of the socalled intelligent design movement, which assumes that the complexity of the cosmos and life can best be explained as the work of an "intelligent designer" rather than by evolutionary theory.

In the hypothetical case that the big bang would reoccur, according to Stephen Hawking, it's highly unlikely that the same universe as ours would emerge from it. And as we saw earlier, Darwin's theory of evolution by natural selection is based on stochastic processes with an undeterminable outcome. This indicates anything but a preconceived plan.

For millions of years, our distant ancestors faced life-threatening natural phenomena. Consider harsh climatic conditions such as ice ages and long periods of extreme drought or rain. But also volcanic eruptions and shifting tectonic plates threatened the survival of species. We saw earlier that sixty-six million years ago, the dinosaurs became extinct as a result of the impact of an asteroid in Mexico, after having dominated planet earth for two hundred million years. By the way, some flying dinosaurs, from which our birds are descended, were able to survive this disaster. Suppose this lump of rock had missed the earth at the time, it is not out of the question that Jurassic Park would have existed millions of years longer. And had our distant ancestors not survived this dino era, *Homo sapiens* would never have existed. If, however, this asteroid had collided with the earth a little earlier or a little later, then this chunk of rock would not have crashed on the rocky bottom of Yucatan, but would have splashed somewhere into the Atlantic or Pacific Ocean, respectively. Apart from the fact that this would have triggered a gigantic tsunami, the impact on planet earth would have been very different and possibly the dinosaurs could have survived this scenario. Clearly, our distant ancestors managed to endure severe hardships over time, but without the luck factor, they would have long since become extinct.

Creationists assume that a creator set the constants of nature *a priori* so that nearly *fourteen billion years later (!)* man could thrive on planet earth. But a creator could not have known in advance, unless supernaturally omniscient, how many stars would appear and whether at least one single bio-friendly planet would orbit any of those stars at all. And even if this were the case, it was by no means certain that humans would also have appeared there. After all, we saw above that several situations occurred during the evolutionary process in which the survival of our ancestors was a dime a dozen. Had that dime fallen the wrong way, man would not have appeared on the scene. It is therefore utterly implausible that a creator, religious or otherwise, in a process of nearly fourteen billion years with a completely uncertain outcome, purposefully intended to create man. Therefore, only one conclusion is possible:

> Mankind is an unintended by-product of the big bang, and therefore not part of a cosmic plan.

WHAT IS THE MEANING OF LIFE?

This question has been asked by many philosophers in the past. On the one hand, there are pessimists and nihilists like Arthur Schopenhauer (1788–1860) and Friedrich Nietzsche (1844–1900) who argue that there is nothing that makes life worth living. On the other side are the optimists who believe in a God and an afterlife, and put their lives here on earth at the service of a supernatural power. In the middle of the spectrum, we find philosophers such as Jean-Paul Sartre (1905–1980) and Albert Camus (1913–1960), authors of existentialism, who argue that while there is no meaningful authority outside mankind; mankind has the ability to determine its own meaning of life. The philosopher Bertrand Russell says: "Unless you assume a God, the question of life's meaning is meaningless."[3]

As far as I'm concerned, the question—What's the meaning of life?—is an annoying, compulsive one, because this phrase leads to a dead end. It suggests that there is only one, and only one, tenable answer possible for everyone. Why couldn't more versions of the meaning of life be possible? Why shouldn't the meaning of life be something personal? And why shouldn't you be allowed to adjust the meaning of life with advancing insight?

If you ask any person the question—What's the meaning of life?—they're likely to be unable to provide an answer, even though the answer to that question could provide them with certainty and guidance. People have jumped off rooftops because they could no longer see the meaning of life. In that sense, asking that question can make life even more problematic than it already is.

3. Seachris, *Exploring the Meaning of Life*, 83.

Answering the Big Questions

Knowing that mankind is an unintended by-product of the big bang, you shouldn't hang around waiting for a higher power to come and whisper the meaning of life to you. So all that remains is that you, and every human being, must take responsibility for making up your own mind about the meaning of your own life; in other words, the meaning of life is the meaning you give to it yourself. However, man is not alone in life, but is part of a community or society, and therefore he cannot determine the meaning of life in glorious solitude. First, there are the national and local laws that a person has to abide by. Second, there are the practical ethical rules that characterize a community or society, and to which a person has to conform. Leading these are the precepts of the relevant religion, for a person with a belief.

> You can, no, you must decide the meaning of your life for yourself, but always within legal, ethical and, if applicable, religious boundaries.

WHERE DO WE GO FROM HERE?

This question is answered differently by each of the three Abrahamic religions, but as we can't determine whether these religions can coexist or whether only one religion prevails, the answer to this question is a little complicated. Man's ultimate destiny depends on the following conditions:

1. Does God exist at all?
2. Are you religious or a nonbeliever?
3. Are you Jewish, Christian, or Muslim?
4. Have you led a virtuous or an immoral life?

Let's start with the first condition because it can be answered simply: if God doesn't exist, then the nonbelievers had it right. That's bad luck for the believers. After death, it's over and out for everyone. Apparently, God was an idol after all. However, should

God exist, we are left with a three-dimensional puzzle, which I have pictured in the following flowcharts:

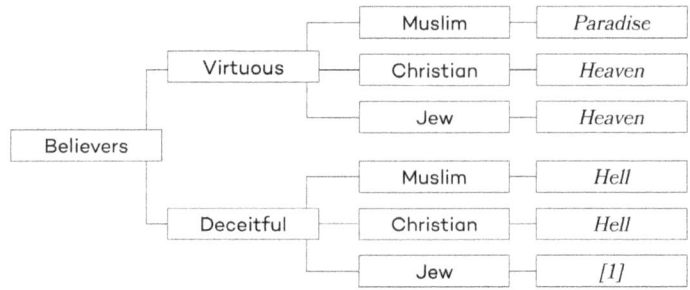

Figure 6. The fate of believers.

[1] *Jews believe in a hell in which a temporary purification process takes place, after which a soul still enters heaven. This applies to Jews and non-Jews alike. Only exceptionally evil people, like Hitler, are doomed to spend their time eternally in hell.*

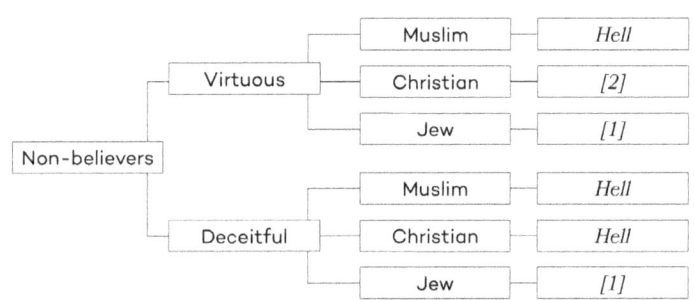

Figure 7. The fate of non-believers.

[2] *For nonbelievers who have led a virtuous life, purgatory or hell basically remain after death, but perhaps there is still a glimmer of hope. The precepts of the Ten Commandments are so general that someone could have lived according to them without knowing these rules. If then, as a nonbeliever, you have intuitively lived according to the Ten Commandments, perhaps God will be merciful and there may still be a place for you—somewhere on the back row in heaven.*

Answering the Big Questions

Notes to the flow charts

There's a widespread misconception that non-Muslims go to Muslim hell. According to the Qur'an, anyone who believes in God and has lived virtuously can go to heaven, regardless of the name of the faith: "Surely those who believe, and those who are Jews, and the Christians, and the Sabians, whoever believes in God and the Last Day and does good, they have their reward with their Lord, and there is no fear for them, nor shall they be grieved." (Q Al-Baqarah 2:62).[4] However, Surah 3:85 states that if someone has a religion other than Islam, this person will not be accepted by Allah: "And whoever seeks a religion other than the Islam, it will not be accepted from him, and in the Hereafter he will be one of the losers." (Q Ali'Imran 3:85).[5]

Nobody knows whether the three Abrahamic Gods coexist, or whether only one God prevails. As shown in the flowcharts, it makes quite a difference for the deceased whether that is Allah, Yahweh, or the God of the Christians. Which God takes the lead here? It's like the quiz "which of the three?" Or will it be "none of the three?"

The French philosopher and mathematician Blaise Pascal (1623–1662) thought it was best to convert to God. If God exists, you at least have a chance of going to heaven and not to hell. And if God does not exist, you will suffer the same fate as all those nonbelievers. According to Pascal, this strategy offers the most optimal result, without knowing whether God exists or not. However, he does not tell you which God you should turn to, so that heaven will pass you by if you have bet on the wrong God.

---

4. Ali, *Koran*, 87.
5. Ali, *Koran*, 127.

9

The End of the Universe

ONE MIGHT WONDER WHAT is going to happen to the earth and the universe in future, assuming that any creator does not interfere with our universe:

THE FATE OF PLANET EARTH

The sun is currently about 4.6 billion years old, with another 5–6 billion years to go. This nuclear furnace, 150 million kilometers away, converts six hundred million tons of hydrogen per second into helium![1] It's now possible to calculate exactly when the sun will have burned all the hydrogen from its core. It will then start burning helium, which is converted into heavier elements like oxygen, carbon and iron, causing it to cool and swell, turning it from a yellow star into a red giant. Next, the earth's atmosphere will be swallowed up and the temperature will rise to the extent that our oceans will evaporate. Furthermore, the sun will swell even more and "consumes" the nearest planets, Mercury and Venus. Our earth is then next to go. Finally, the sun will become so unstable that due to its own gravity, it will implode. By then, all life on earth will have long since been destroyed.

1. Russell, "Solar Furnace."

The End of the Universe

But there's another danger lurking. It's highly likely that our Milky Way is going to collide with the Andromeda Nebula. This galaxy, quite similar to our own galaxy, is coming our way at a speed of 400,000 km/hour.[2] With present-day knowledge, scientists calculate this collision to happen in about four billion years. Due to the enormous distances between them, it's not thought that the stars and planets of both galaxies will effectively collide, but rather that they'll be shaken up considerably by the gravitational pull between them. Hydrogen from both galaxies will come together and form the birthplace for an explosion of new stars. Black holes will seek each other at the center of these merging galaxies. This *cosmic crash* will cause the temperature on earth to rise so high that the oceans boil dry and the earth's surface is scorched. All life on earth will then be irrevocably destroyed. But . . . will humans live to see this end? Some real dangers threaten humanity before the Andromeda Nebula arrives:

An Asteroid Collision

Some sixty-six million years ago, an asteroid about ten to fifteen kilometers in diameter collided with the earth, on Mexico's Yucatan Peninsula to be precise. As a result, 75 percent of the plant and the animal population,[3] including all non-avian dinosaurs, was eventually wiped out. It is a statistical certainty that sometime in the next one hundred million years a similar collision will occur, possibly with even greater impact. This could wipe out our entire civilization. However, mankind is not going to sit and wait for this to happen. On 24 November 2021, NASA, the space agency, sent a spacecraft called DART (*Double Asteroid Redirection Test*) to a pair of asteroids circling somewhere between Mars and Jupiter. The NASA mission was a hit. On 27 September 2022, DART collided with one of the asteroids at 22,000 km/hour causing it to change

---

2. Drake, "Our Galaxy Is Due."
3. Wei-Haas, "Last Day."

orbit. This means that in future, we can arm ourselves against an asteroid impact, provided the asteroid is not too big.

Habitat Self-Destruction

Over time, *Homo sapiens* have managed to become the most dominant species on planet earth. As a result, we can be compared to a plague of rabbits, and like rabbits, we are defiling our own lair, pardon, the globe. However, this has dramatic consequences, which we are currently experiencing firsthand. Don't say we didn't see it coming! A contemporary of Charles Darwin, the Anglican preacher Thomas Malthus (1766–1834), warned against overpopulation, even in his day. His reasoning was that if the population increased exponentially, the growth of food production, which he believed was linear, would be unable to keep pace with the increase in population, resulting in widespread famine. The Club of Rome reiterated this prediction in 1972 with its report *The Limits to Growth*.[4] Still, our "naked ape" instinct to keep on reproducing wins out over reason. As the consequences of overpopulation become abundantly clear in the form of climate change, politicians are now taking action. However, as often is the case in politics, it's "locking the stable door—after the horse has bolted!" Overpopulation is the true structural problem, the current CO_2 policy, though necessary, is merely symptom control.

And, in addition to the population explosion, the gap between rich and poor continues to widen. This theme has been exhaustively described by French economist Thomas Piketty (1971–present). However, the success of his books has made him part of the problem. Furthermore, religious tensions between nations and geopolitical tensions can escalate at any time and cruelly disrupt world order. And, as recently experienced, pandemics are constantly with us. It's not inconceivable that one day a deadly virus will emerge that mutates so rapidly that no vaccine can counter

---

4. Meadows, *Limits to Growth*.

it. The result will be the decimation of mankind, as happened during the plague epidemic in the Middle Ages.

Nuclear War

A nuclear war, both global and regional, is not imaginary. At the time of writing, tensions between the US and Russia as a result of the war in Ukraine have flared up to such an extent that the danger of a nuclear war has become a reality. The US and Russia possess enough nuclear weapons to destroy literally everything on earth. Besides the many fatalities, the consequences for those remaining will be dramatic. A nuclear war will spread huge amounts of particulate matter in the atmosphere, blocking sunlight and thus making the world darker and colder. Researchers have recently discovered that under these conditions, a significant part of the ozone layer may disappear. After a few years—when the smoke clears and temperatures will start rising again—UV radiation will increase dramatically with far-reaching consequences for the biotope's health. This is not something to look forward to. We can only hope that politicians will persevere with their endeavors to eliminate nuclear weapons worldwide.

The Development of Artificial Intelligence

Since the advent of ChatGPT, the discussion about artificial intelligence (AI) has flared up again. Besides AI's almost limitless opportunities for good, there's also a dangerous downside, and this is by no means science fiction. Just before his death in 2018, Stephen Hawking pointed out the dangers of AI: "The primitive forms of artificial intelligence we already have, have proved very useful. But I think that the development of full artificial intelligence could spell the end of the human race. Once humans develop artificial intelligence, it would take off on its own and redesign itself at an ever-increasing rate. Humans, who are limited by slow biological evolution, can't compete and will be superseded."[5]

In summary:

1. AI systems are self-learning.
2. AI systems learn faster than humans.
3. In time, AI systems will surpass human intelligence.
4. And according to Hawking, the punch line: AI systems can start setting goals which conflict with ours.

That's when all hell breaks loose. It takes little fantasy to imagine the calamities this could lead to. And once AI systems are equipped with quantum computers, these dangers, and their consequences, will gain momentum at an exponential pace.

Here is Hawking's bold statement:

> In short, the advent of super-intelligent AI would be either the best or the worst thing ever to happen to humanity.[6]

Escape to Mars

Billionaire entrepreneurs Bezos, Branson, and Musk want to get ahead of all this doom, and they're already planning to travel to Mars. In the meantime they've reached the stage of offering space travel, at considerable cost, to the happy few, as of course, they are businessmen. They also see economic opportunities with relocations to Mars in the future, but for them money does not play a role. They are looking for fame and glory because whoever wins this space race will go down in history as the new Columbus. There's a slight difference though: when Columbus set off from Portugal in 1492, he didn't even know he was going to discover America!

---

5. Evergreen, *Autonomous Transformation*, 117.
6. Hawking, *Brief Answers*, 188.

The End of the Universe

The End Is Inevitable

It's inevitable that within five to six billion years, the sun will burn out, making life on earth impossible. However, before that happens, the temperature on earth will have risen so much due to the dying sun that mankind will not survive. Also, it doesn't seem like a good idea for man to wait for the Andromeda Nebula to collide with the Milky Way, because man would not survive this cosmic crash either. Anyway, man will be doomed to hop from planet to planet as the corresponding stars die out. But even then, the "universal gypsies" will eventually have to capitulate, well before the last day of the universe has arrived.

WHAT WILL HAPPEN NEXT?

Below, I've described three common scenarios in which our universe could come to an end:

Gravity Wins Out over Expansion

The universe continues to expand, but at some point, this expansion comes to a halt and it then starts to contract to end in the *big crunch*.[7] In this scenario, gravity conquers "dark energy." As the retraction progresses, galaxies get closer and closer to each other and collisions like the one described above occur—the possible collision of the Andromeda Nebula with our Milky Way. At the end of this contraction, the universe is compressed into a point of infinite density, a singularity. The universe is back to square one.

Expansion Wins out Over Gravity

The universe continues to expand because the expanding force exceeds the power of gravity. To help you understand, imagine that space consists only of the spherical surface of a big balloon, with

---

7. "Big Crunch."

galaxies scattered all over its surface. If the balloon is inflated further, space is created and the galaxies get further and further apart, so much so that eventually light can no longer reach the neighboring galaxies. If you then look into a telescope, you'll no longer see anything; it will get lonely on those planets. But the story gets even worse. At some point, the surrounding gas clouds will run out and no more new stars can be formed. Those stars that still exist, will extinguish and the temperature will drop to zero degrees Kelvin. This end state is called the *big chill* or the *big freeze*.[8]

Expansion Runs Wild

For billions of years, the expansion of the universe was relatively slow, but, since 1998, the expansion has picked up at an ever increasing speed. Scientists from Vanderbilt University in Tennessee have developed a model, in which the expansion of the universe accelerates at such a rate that in the end, individual atoms are ripped apart.[9] According to this mathematical model, called the *big rip*, all the material in the universe will be torn apart twenty-two billion years from now; sixty million years before the end, the stars in our galaxy will be driven apart. Three months before the end, the planets of our solar system will be driven into space. Half an hour before the end, our earth will explode. And, a fraction of a second before the end, all atoms will be ripped apart.

Further to these three scenarios, there are several other theories about how the universe might end, but that's all outside the scope of this book. Which scenario eventually will take place is difficult to predict. The uncertainty in making a prediction is related to dark matter and dark energy as physicists are currently unable to accurately assess their behavior. But let's stop here, after all, mankind will be long gone by then.

8. "Future of an Expanding Universe."
9. "New Model of Cosmic Stickiness."

10

The Future of the Universe

I HOPE THAT AFTER reading the previous chapter, you'll be able to recover from the shock of mankind's fate! However, there's a glimmer of hope on the horizon in the sense that there might be a chance for the rebirth of the universe. We're now entering the realm of speculation and fantasy, which is quite refreshing after the cold death of the *big chill*, the inferno of the *big crunch,* or the slaughter by the *big rip*. The big question, however, is whether mankind will also return in this rebirth.

Let's start with a thought experiment.

Now suppose our universe ends in the *big crunch*, i.e., in a singularity. There's a universal unwritten law that says that if something can happen in nature, it will happen. We commonly refer to *Murphy's Law*—if something can go wrong, it will go wrong, a variation on this universal law. It is widely accepted that the big bang actually occurred. Assuming that any creator would not interfere with our universe, it follows that the big bang was not an "act of God," but a natural phenomenon. According to the unwritten law, something similar to this big bang can and will happen again, so that a new universe would be created. This new universe will probably, one day, implode again into a singularity. Thereafter, history will continue to repeat itself, and this *ad infinitum*. Whether mankind will reappear in any of these universes is the big question, which depends on whether similar cosmic conditions reoccur. Stephen Hawking was not optimistic: "The odds against a universe that has produced life like ours are immense."[1] Here, Hawking is probably referring to the fact that, partly due to quantum and other random effects, the big bang is not a deterministic process. Therefore, it is by no means certain that mankind would reappear on the scene.

Along that same line of reasoning, you come to the conclusion that before our universe, another universe must have existed. And another one before that. One might wonder if there ever was a very first universe. Then there must also have been a very first big bang. But who caused the very first big bang? Was this the ultimate creator? And then, who created the ultimate creator? But as with our universe, time stood still and no creator could exist. And as with our universe, it didn't take anyone at all to push the button of the very first big bang. Therefore, before the very first universe there existed an even older universe and before that another one. Viewed this way, the history and future of our universe is a perpetual harmonica-movement of expansions and contractions: a cyclic universe. Since the total amount of mass/energy in this closed system always remains the same, and therefore the first law of thermodynamics is satisfied, the cyclic universe is in fact an everlasting perpetuum mobile.

Let's go one step further. Now suppose that this everlasting, cyclic universe actually exists. That means that if you just wait long enough, infinitely many universes will appear and disappear. Then there is a chance that a bio-friendly universe (a universe with at least one bio-friendly planet) will pass by. And precisely in such a bio-friendly universe we could currently find ourselves. This would then be, similar to the explanation from the multiverse theory, an alternative explanation for the fine-tuning argument.

Let me stop fantasizing and speculating here. Our universe is currently still expanding, and it expands even faster the further away you look. In fact, astronomers discovered in 1998 that the expansion of the universe was even speeding up. Therefore, for

---

1. Ferguson, *Stephen Hawking*, 131.

The Future of the Universe

now, nothing points to a Big Crunch scenario, including a cyclical universe. However, astronomers cannot explain the acceleration of the universe. This has everything to do with the mysterious nature and workings of dark matter and dark energy. Consequently, the way our universe comes to an end remains shrouded in mists.

There are certain reasons to believe that other so-called parallel universes could exist outside our universe. First, on metaphysical grounds, this would be a parallel universe in which God resides. It's obvious to assume that this parallel universe is not finite in time, but eternal. Then there are several theoretical-physical arguments for the existence of a multiverse. For instance, not so long ago, Stephen Hawking and Thomas Hertog concluded that from the Hartle–Hawking model (see appendix 5), which is based on quantum physics, a multiverse logically and inevitably must emerge. The renowned American string theorist, Brian Greene (1963–present) also concludes that from M-theory, a multiverse must emerge.

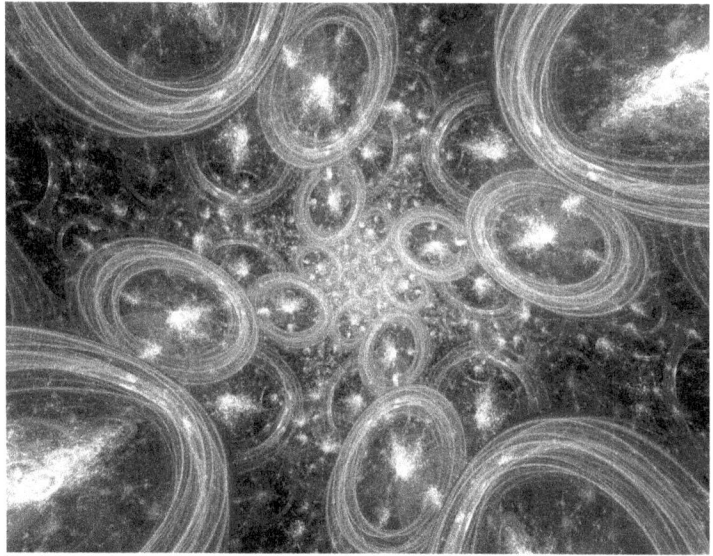

©Alamy, 2016
Figure 8. The multi-bubble universe.

Another example is the multi-bubble theory proposed by the American physicist Paul Steinhardt (1952–present). Steinhardt surmises that just after the big bang, inflation kept stopping in one area, and continuing in another area. All these separate bubbles, as they are called, evolved into parallel universes that moved increasingly far apart. A prerequisite for the existence of this multi-bubble universe is, of course, that the hyperinflation actually did occur. If not, the concept of infinite bubble creation can be consigned to the scientific dustbin. However, the fact that the multiverse inevitably emerges from certain theoretical models does not mean that it really exists at all. The problem here is that, practically spoken, we cannot make observations outside our own universe, as must have become clear in chapter 6. And, as philosopher of science Karl Popper (1902–1994) rightly states, a theory that cannot be verified or falsified is not a scientific theory.

To Close

I WISH I WAS religious, but, despite my strict Catholic upbringing, that's simply not me. If I were religious, I could draw comfort and hope from my faith in bad times. Moreover, with good behavior, I could look forward to eternal life after death. However, as a nonbeliever, I'll simply have to make do with my temporary existence on this globe, with perhaps a sequel in hell. But I'm not completely ruling out the possibility that God exists. I am, like everyone else for that matter, agnostic.

On 25 December 2021, the James Webb Space Telescope was launched to replace the old Hubble Space Telescope. This new telescope, the size of a tennis court, is many times more powerful and orbits the sun 1.5 million kilometers from planet earth. On 11 July 2022, President Joe Biden proudly revealed the first images, in high resolution, to the world. This highly complex, technological feat could have gone wrong in any number of ways, but the space telescope seems to be functioning perfectly. And that's just as well, because the James Webb project will over its lifetime cost around $14 billion. That's one dollar for every year the universe has existed! Astrophysicists really don't care about this, and they're eagerly awaiting the upcoming infrared images that will take us back in time to more than thirteen billion years ago, allowing us to learn more about the origins of the universe.

So, what else does physics have to offer?

Physicists on the front lines are working hard to unify the theory of the macrocosm (theory of relativity) and the microcosm (quantum physics). Albert Einstein and Stephen Hawking had fervently hoped that during their lifetimes they would live to see this holy grail of physics, the "theory of everything" become reality. Sadly for them, it was not to be. One of the promising candidates for the "theory of everything" is the so-called string theory. If this theory ever succeeds in unifying the four fundamental forces, it might be possible to make better predictions about the evolution of the universe, perhaps clarifying obscure issues such as "black holes," "dark matter," and "dark energy." We would then also be able to predict with greater certainty which theory for the end of our universe is most likely. The physicist who first succeeds in describing the "theory of everything" will become the new Einstein. In reality, it is likely to be a joint effort of several physicists, as happened with quantum physics. Simultaneously with the search for the "theory of everything," the next question is already sounding: did God play a role in the creation of the laws of nature?

Whatever happens, these are exciting times for physicists. The bullet train of physics thunders on while the boat of philosophy moves slowly, and the horse-drawn tram of religions remains at a standstill. Natural science will increasingly continue to take territory from philosophy and religion. If, in this regard, I had to make a prediction, it's not inconceivable that, not far from now, a generally accepted solution to the body-spirit problem will emerge in favor of the monists. More precisely, I'm in the camp of physicalists who assume that all the rational, moral, and psychological thoughts and feelings of human beings arise from physiological processes in the brain and are explainable from natural science. Meanwhile, today, by measuring brain activity, one can detect, for example, what specific song a person is thinking about. It is not inconceivable that in future it will even be possible to measure brain activity at the level of individual neurons. Obviously, our thought processes cannot exist without our brain. After all, information cannot exist without an information carrier. When an information carrier is destroyed, the information stored on it is no longer reproducible. When we die and our brain ceases to function, all the information stored in it is also no longer reproducible. Hence, there is no spirit that can go to the afterlife after death, which contradicts the version of the Old Testament. Is this a problem? Not for philosophy it seems to me. The dualists were apparently wrong. For philosophers among us, there's still plenty of food for thought. But for religions, damage done is considerable. If the spirit does die with the body, what then goes to the afterlife? It seems to me that God has a serious problem to solve here.

In our search, we have not come across any evidence for the existence of God. However, with present-day knowledge, we can conclude the following:

1. The creation and evolution of both the universe and mankind was a spontaneous, autonomous process that did not involve God.
2. God did not even intend to create man; mankind is an unintended by-product of the big bang.
3. The only possible role left for God concerns the creation of the laws of nature. But if the laws of nature evolved simultaneously with the big bang, what Stephen Hawking, Thomas Hertog, and other leading physicists suspect, then there's no longer any room for God to have acted as the creator. Then natural science is done with God. What then is the relevance of God?

In addition, there are countless other arguments against God. Just check out the books by Richard Dawkins (*The God Delusion*), Christopher Hitchens (*God is Not Great*), and Victor Stenger (*God: The Failed Hypothesis*). It's therefore tempting to conclude that God does not exist, but I think that that's too easy. After all, the answer to the question of whether or not a metaphysical being exists is, by definition, beyond the realm of natural science. This is precisely why science cannot rule out the existence or nonexistence of God, any more than we cannot rule out the existence or nonexistence of the Flying Spaghetti Monster, scientifically speaking. Only, in the case of the Flying Spaghetti Monster, everyone will agree that it is nonsense. Either way, the question of whether God exists or

God Yes? God No?

is just an imaginary being created by the human interpretive urge remains unanswered for now. Conclusion:

> Theists cannot prove that God exists, and atheists cannot prove that God does not exist.

As long as this is the case, both camps will undoubtedly continue their polemics. We can, however, judge the acts attributed to God, which fall within the realm of natural science, on their scientific merits and possibly disprove them. This was the primary purpose of my writing.

As natural science advances, it will get closer and closer to truth, but the mere fact that the universe exists at all will probably remain a mystery.

Why is there something rather than nothing?[1]

According to the German philosopher and mathematician Gottfried Wilhelm von Leibniz (1646–1716), this is the ultimate question mankind should ask. Until this primordial existential question is answered, we cannot rule out the existence of God. Or am I making the time-honored classical mistake here of putting the stamp of God on an unsolved mystery?

It therefore seems appropriate to end with a quote from Shakespeare's Hamlet: "There are more things in heaven and earth, Horatio, than are dreamt of in your philosophy."[2]

---

1. Dascal, Leibniz, 452.
2. Shakespeare, *Hamlet*, 143.

APPENDIX 1

Isaac Newton

Isaac Newton: The Father of Classical Mechanics

THE ENGLISHMAN ISAAC NEWTON, inventor of the law of gravitation, is one of the greatest physicists of all time. Legend has it that Newton came up with his ideas about gravity when he saw an apple fall from a tree in his mother's orchard. He then came to realize that gravity could extend far beyond the apple tree, for example . . . to the moon! Later, he was able to exactly calculate the moon's orbit around the earth.

LadyofHats, 2012
Figure 9. Newton under the apple tree.

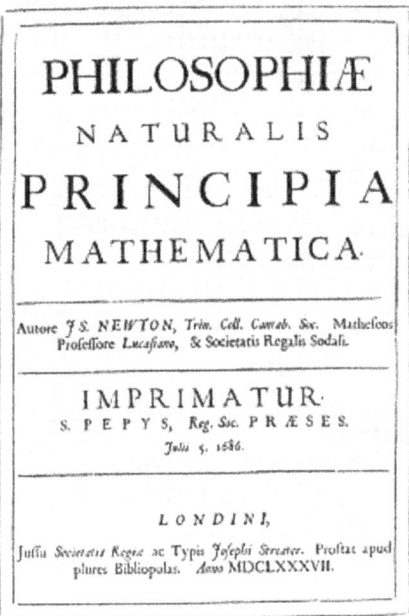

S. Pepys, 1686
Figure 10. Newton's famous book.

Isaac Newton

As a professor of mathematics at Cambridge University, he formulated the laws of motion in his book *Philosophiæ Naturalis Principia Mathematica* (Mathematical Principles of Natural Philosophy), first published in 1687. A brief summary of the laws:

1. *First law*: An object to which no force is applied moves at a constant speed in a straight line or is at rest. This law formulates the inertia of an object.

2. *Second law*: The force exerted on an object is equal to the product of the mass of the object and the acceleration the object undergoes. This law, in formula form $F = m \times a$, is the main law of classical mechanics, in which

    "F" is force,
    "m" is mass,
    "a" is acceleration.

3. *Third law*: If an object A exerts a force on object B, then object B simultaneously exerts the same but opposite force on object A. This law is known as "action = reaction."

Newton's Law of Gravitation

In addition to the laws of motion, Newton devised the law of gravitation, which defines the force by which two masses attract each other. This force is directed along the line connecting both centers of gravity, and is proportional to the product of the two masses, and inversely proportional to the square of their distance.

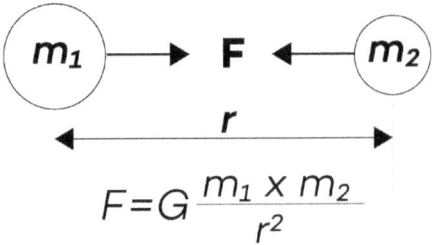

Figure 11. Newton's law of gravitation.

"F" is the gravitational force,
"G" is the gravitational constant,
"m1" is the first mass,
"m2" is the second mass,
"r" is the distance between the centers of gravity of the two masses.

Newton assumed a worldview of absolute space and time. He used one three-dimensional coordinate system in which all events occurred simultaneously. Every movement was the result of a cause. Newton could calculate exactly how fast an apple would fall from a tree or where a cannonball would land. But he was also able to describe the orbit of the planets around the sun. At the time, it was thought that with this deterministic system, theoretical physics would soon be complete. However, two centuries later, it turned out that classical mechanics, unlike general relativity, would not be able to accurately describe, for example, Mercury's orbit around the sun.

Although Newton's law of gravitation enabled him to accurately calculate the orbits of the other planets, he had the greatest difficulty with the idea of "action at a distance." In a letter to the philologist Richard Bentley, he wrote: "That gravity should be innate inherent and essential to matter so that one body may act upon another at a distance through a vacuum without the mediation of any thing else by and through which their action or force may be conveyed from one to another is to me so great an absurdity that I believe no man who has in philosophical matters any competent faculty or thinking can ever fall into it."[1] So his greatest frustration was that he was never able to fathom the essence of gravity, or in his own words: "I have not as yet been able to deduce from phenomena the reason for these properties of gravity, and I do not feign hypotheses."[2] Put more simply, Newton didn't understand the essence of his own theory. With today's knowledge, we know that Newton could never have solved this problem by himself. That required, two centuries later, the brilliant mind of a certain Einstein.

Godfrey Kneller, 1689

Isaac Newton (1642–1727)

Isaac Newton was not only a physicist, but also a philosopher, mathematician, astronomer, theologian, and alchemist. More or less simultaneously, the German mathematician Gottfried Wilhelm von Leibniz (1646–1716), apart from Newton, developed differential and integral calculus. Alongside the *Principia*

---

1. Debrock and Schreurer, *Newton's Scientific and Philosophical Legacy*, 52.
2. Newton, *Principia*, 276.

Mathematica, Newton published *Opticks*, in which he described his optical experiments, as well as the conclusions about the workings of light. To do so, Newton used a mirror telescope he had invented himself. In 1696, he moved from Cambridge to London to take up the honorable post of master of the mint. In this capacity, he ensured the transition of the English pound from the silver to the gold standard. For his work as mint master, he was knighted by Queen Anne of England in 1705 and was henceforth *Sir* Isaac Newton.

Newton was the only son of a wealthy farmer of the same name, who died shortly before Isaac's birth. As a premature baby, it was thought that Isaac would not survive. However, he did, and a few years after his birth, his mother remarried and left young Newton's upbringing to his grandmother. This experience left an indelible impression on Newton, which manifested itself in later life through insecure, irrational behavior and depression. In particular, his constant battle with his main scientific opponent, Robert Hooke (1635–1703), who accused him of plagiarism regarding the law of gravitation and optics, drove Newton to extreme outbursts of anger. Gottfried Wilhelm von Leibniz, who independently of Newton had also developed differential and integral calculus, also accused him of plagiarism, but Newton, as president of the Royal Society, could easily parry this attack.

Despite his fame, Newton's private life was far from perfect. He was an unpleasant person, never married, had few friends, and was basically a loner. He was deeply religious and much of his life was occupied with theological questions. He wrote: "I have a fundamental belief in the Bible as the Word of God, written by those who were inspired. I study the Bible daily."[3] In March 1727, Newton suffered severe stomach pains and died, aged 84. After his death, his fame continued to grow. According to a 1905 poll among the members of the Royal Society, Newton was designated as the greatest scholar in the entire history of science, even greater than Albert Einstein.

---

3. Stvarnik, *Portraits of the Great*, 135.

Appendix 2

Charles Darwin

CHARLES DARWIN COLLECTED VAST amounts of biological material during his voyage on the ship HMS *Beagle*, including plants, fossils, and animals, as well as all kinds of rocks—he had also studied geology. While at Cambridge University, Darwin may not have been the best student, but he was an excellent observer. On his return to England after five years, he documented everything he had collected on his trip. Twenty years later, he published his famous book *On the Origin of Species by Means of Natural Selection or the Preservation of Favoured Races in the Struggle for Life*. Although a mouthful, this title represents the core of his theory of evolution. Let's go through the evolutionary process step by step:

1. First, Darwin observed that in any population of organisms of the same species, there is great variety. No organism is the same.
2. From his contemporary Thomas Malthus (1766–1834), he had understood that not all organisms survive; there is a struggle for life.
3. Organisms best adapted to their environment are most likely to survive.
4. Finally, inheritance must occur of those traits that contribute to survival.

Further clarification:

1. Spontaneous changes in genetic material (mutations) create variations in the population.
2. A small difference in appearance or behavior can make the difference between life and death.
3. Individuals within a population do not change, the composition of the population changes.
4. Natural selection is not a purposive process. Only in retrospect can one understand and explain how natural selection occurred.
5. Evolution is a gradual process over a long period.
6. The favorable traits must be anchored in the DNA, otherwise inheritance, i.e. evolution, does not work.
7. The evolutionary process never stops.

Unknown artist
Figure 12. Cartoon titled "Man is but a worm."

I'll illustrate this with an example of the evolutionary process in action: on a volcanic island with gray-brown rocks, a bird with slightly dark-tinged feathers is not as easily spotted by its natural enemies as its lighter-toned conspecific, and therefore has a better chance of survival. This phenomenon is what Darwin called "natural selection." Consequently, relatively more birds with slightly dark-tinged feathers survive. When these birds reproduce, the next generation will have slightly more dark-tinged feathers than the previous one. This process of gradual change continues from generation to generation, until eventually, the population has a camouflage color that matches the color of the volcanic rock.

The Evolutionary Process in a Diagram

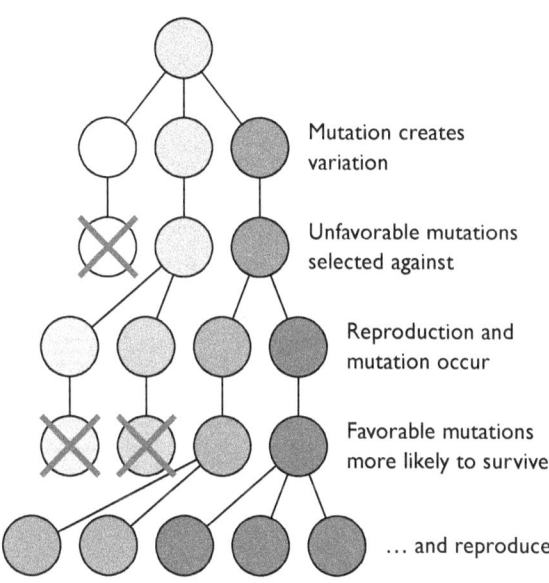

Elembis, 2007
Figure 13. Natural selection of a population.

Darwin used the term "survival of the fittest" to refer to the result of "natural selection." However, he didn't coin this term himself; he took it from the British economist Herbert Spencer (1820–1903). Now, it's never a great idea to blindly adopt statements by economists, and in this case too, it leads to misinterpretations. The term "survival of the fittest" is understood by many as "survival of the strongest" or "survival of the smartest" or something along those lines, and that's precisely not what Darwin intended. What Darwin meant by "natural selection" was that organisms that are best adapted to their environment or to changing conditions have the best chances of survival. It would have been better if Darwin had referred to natural selection as "survival of the best adapters."

Organisms that survive are not stronger or smarter than their peers that didn't make it, they have simply inherited the right characteristics to survive. Or in Darwin's own words:

> "It is not the strongest of the species that survives, nor the most intelligent that survives, it is the one that is most adaptable to change."[1]

Riddle

Darwin's theory of evolution also made it possible to solve the chicken-and-egg problem. The most elegant formulation came from renowned American astrophysicist Neil deGrasse Tyson: "Which came first the chicken or the egg?" His answer: "The egg—laid by a bird that was not itself a chicken."[2] According to the biblical creation story, the chicken was there first. As both statements cannot be true at the same time, please make your own choice!

1. Brown, *Darwin*, 54.
2. Tyson, "Just to Settle It."

T. H. Maguire, 1849

Charles Darwin (1809–1882)

Charles Darwin was born into a family of doctors, and it was obvious that he would also follow this tradition. However, during his studies, he reportedly discovered that he couldn't face blood, so he dropped out of medical school. His father then determined that Charles should become a priest. While studying theology, the twenty-two-year-old Charles was invited to travel around the world on the sailing ship HMS *Beagle*, an opportunity he gratefully accepted. Wherever he went, he studied the local fauna and flora. He collected huge quantities of animals, skeletons, plants, fossils, and geological objects and had them sent back to England.

The best example of "natural selection" he found were the finches he collected from the Galapagos Islands in the Pacific Ocean, about a thousand kilometers off the coast of Ecuador. He initially went to the Galapagos Islands to study the turtle population; the finches were really an extra.

1. Geospiza magnirostris
2. Geospiza fortis
3. Geospiza parvula
4. Certhidea olivacea

Pinzones de las islas Galápagos

John Gould
Figure 14. Darwin's finches.

On his return to England, he donated the bird collection to the Zoological Society of London. John Gould (1804–1881), an ornithologist attached to this institute, quickly saw that they were different species, belonging to the same finch family. Certain morphological characteristics, but especially the shape of the bill, were associated by Darwin with the different types of food found on the various islands. For instance, finches that ate mainly insects developed a pointed beak, and finches that lived on nuts or seeds developed a powerful, blunted beak. Five of Darwin's finches can still be admired at the Naturalis Biodiversity Center in Leiden, Netherlands.

His journey was initially supposed to take two years, but the *Beagle* eventually arrived back in England three years later than planned. Back in Cambridge, Darwin began to analyze and classify the huge mountain of collected material—this took him the rest of his life. He described his observations and the theory of evolution extensively and meticulously in his book *On the Origin of Species*; he referred to the five hundred pages as "a first summary."

It's unfair to give Darwin all the credit for developing the theory of evolution. He adopted original thoughts from several contemporaries working on the issue. Even his own grandfather, Erasmus Darwin, had developed ideas that anticipated the theory of evolution. In fact, around the same time, the biologist Alfred Russel Wallace (1823–1913) had developed a similar theory of evolution independently of Darwin. When Darwin realized that Wallace was about to publish his theory, he speeded up his work and published *On the Origin of Species* just before Wallace could take credit.

However, there was a fundamental aspect in his own theory of evolution that Darwin could not explain; namely, how the inheritance of the newly acquired traits worked. With today's knowledge, we know that this involves mutations in the DNA code, but this knowledge was unavailable to Darwin. At the same time, a contemporary of Darwin, the monk Gregor Mendel, had developed his theory of heredity, but for some reason, Darwin never took note of it. Thus, he was unable to understand an essential aspect of his own theory, namely the mystery of inheritance.

Although Darwin had studied for priesthood, as he grew older he increasingly began to doubt his faith. He had observed so much cruelty and suffering in nature that he couldn't imagine that God could be its creator. In fact, at the time of writing *On the Origin of Species*, he had already renounced his faith, which put him in a quandary, as his wife was a devout believer. Also, as a biologist/geologist, he obviously knew that his theory of evolution conflicted with the biblical creation story. Toward the end of his life Darwin wrote: "In my most extreme fluctuations I have never been an atheist in the sense of denying the existence of God,—I think that generally (and more and more as I grow older) but not always, that an agnostic would be the most correct description of my state of mind."[3]

In later life, Darwin struggled with chronic health problems, but despite his illness, even after the publication of *On the Origin of Species*, he continued working tirelessly to further develop the theory of evolution, until his death at the age of seventy-three.

---

3. Darwin, Charles Darwin to John Fordyce.

Appendix 3

Albert Einstein

I'LL NOW INTRODUCE YOU to the world of Albert Einstein—one that's very different from how we perceive our everyday world. The rules in his world are different from ours, and you'll probably have some qualms initially. However, in the end, you'll have no choice but to accept Einstein's conclusions, because to date, no physical phenomena have been observed in the macrocosm that contradict his theory of relativity.

> When a man sits with a pretty girl for an hour, it seems like a minute. But let him sit on a hot stove for a minute—and it's longer than any hour. That's relativity.[1]

THE SPECIAL THEORY OF RELATIVITY

Long before Einstein published his special theory of relativity in 1905, the phenomenon of relative speeds was already known. There's no need at all to illustrate this with high speeds—for example, those near the speed of light—as most train passengers have experienced "relative speeds" firsthand, as described in the following example.

---

1. Einstein, quoted in Stefan, *Thus Spoke Einstein*, 441.

Suppose you're in a train traveling at a constant speed of 100 km/hour. Also, suppose there are no objects such as trees, houses and things like that along the railway. This is important because you'd be able to tell from these objects whether or not the train is moving relative to the earth. Furthermore, you have to assume that your train doesn't make any noise.

Let's begin. You're sitting comfortably in your seat and you're neither pushed forward because of the train braking, nor are you pushed backward because of the train accelerating. If you look outside, you have no idea how fast the train is going, because nothing can be seen outside. Thus, your mind could consider the train to be standing still. At one point, your train is overtaken on the parallel track by a fast train, traveling at a constant speed of 150 km/hour. You're still looking outside and you see the fast train passing by at 50 km/hour relative to the speed of your own train, while you feel that your own train is standing still. In contrast, a person sitting in the fast train experiences something different when looking at your train—he sees your train travelling at 50 km/hour but in the opposite direction!

Someone waiting at a level crossing sees your train travelling at 100 km/h and the fast train at 150 km/h, while that fast train is overtaking the ordinary train. An astronaut, whose rocket has now reached an altitude from which the earth's rotation can be observed, looks through his telescope and sees something entirely different.

For convenience, suppose the railway line runs exactly across the equator and both trains, the ordinary and the fast train, are traveling in the earth's direction of rotation. The earth's orbital speed at the equator is 1,667 km/hour. This means that the astronaut sees your train travelling at 1,767 km/hour and the fast train at 1,817 km/ hour. From the astronaut's point of view, the trains are only slowly overtaking each other!

Four people therefore have four completely different perceptions regarding one and the same event. It seems as if the speed of an object can only be determined in relation to another object that's either moving at a constant speed or at rest. But here, Albert

Albert Einstein

Einstein comes into play. He asserts that the speed of light is always and everywhere the same, i.e., independent of the speed of the light source. Or in his own words:

> Light is always propagated in empty space with a definite velocity c which is independent of the state of the emitting body.[2]

The letter "c" (derived from the Latin word *celeritas*, meaning "speed") stands for the speed of light, which is about 300,000 km/sec. Light (in vacuum) circles the earth at the level of the equator more than seven times per second. You'll read further on that Einstein's statement has far-reaching consequences.

As light always takes time to get from A to B, simultaneous events do not exist, from the observer's point of view. For instance, when you watch the sun sinking into the sea, in reality, it has already disappeared below the horizon for about eight minutes, as light has to travel the distance from the sun to the earth, i.e., about 150 million kilometers, at a speed of 300,000 km/sec.

But something extraordinary happens to time at high speeds. This is illustrated with the following experiment performed by Albert Einstein and Belgian astrophysicist Georges Lemaître (1894–1966), the discoverer of the big bang.

---

2. Lehrer and Janssen, *Cambridge Companion to Einstein*, 75.

Albert Einstein

Look closely at this drawing, because herein lies the crux of the special theory of relativity.

Daniël Maas, 2022
Figure 15. Einstein–Lemaître experiment.

Lemaître is standing in his monastery garden and sees a rocket piloted by Einstein shoot past at a gigantic, constant speed. Both Lemaître (on earth) and Einstein (in the rocket) have a light clock that works as follows: between two mirrors A and B, a beam of light goes back and forth. The light beam starts from mirror A, is reflected back by mirror B and, as soon as it returns to mirror A, the clock advances one tick.

In Lemaître's clock, the beam of light returns to the same point from which it departed. From Lemaître's position, something else is happening with Einstein's clock. While the light beam is on its way to mirror B, the rocket travels a certain distance, and therefore the light beam doesn't reach mirror B at the same level as its point of departure.

Conclusion:

1. For Lemaître, time doesn't change.
2. From Lemaître's perspective, Einstein's time slows down.
3. For Einstein, time doesn't change either.

From Lemaître's position, the light in Einstein's clock travels a greater distance than the light in his own clock. Therefore, for Lemaître, Einstein's time must slow down since the speed of light is the same for both.

Unknown photographer, 1933
Figure 16. Meeting between Einstein and Lemaître in 1933.

Einstein could also imagine that the rocket itself is stationary and that the earth below is rotating at great speed. According to the principle of relativity, the outcome remains basically the same; now, from Einstein's perspective, Lemaître's time slows down, whereas his own time does not change. More generally, the relativity principle asserts that it makes no difference whether an observer is at rest or moving at a constant speed in a rectilinear fashion; the laws of nature remain intact. The exact delay, called time dilation, is easily calculated using the Pythagorean theorem, but we'll skip that here. With similar reasoning, it can be shown that the length of the rocket becomes shorter at high speeds (near the speed of light). Thus, from Lemaître's perspective, the rocket appears shorter than it actually is. We'll not discuss this so-called length contraction further here, as this effect isn't relevant to our story.

The special theory of relativity in one sentence:

| At high speeds, time slows down and lengths become shorter.

To be precise, this statement is true from the perspective of observers in steady straight-line motion or at rest, watching objects traveling close to the speed of light.

Unknown photographer, 1931
Figure 17. Einstein explains his famous formula.

Three months after the publication of his special theory of relativity, in 1905, Einstein published a new paper titled "Does the Inertia of an Object Depend Upon its Energy-Content?," which he said was a logical follow-up to his previous publication. Einstein wrote that the answer to that question was a "yes," completely at odds with the general opinion in those days. In the above paper, Einstein already established a connection between energy and mass. Shortly after followed with his famous formula:

| $E = mc^2$

The "E" in the formula stands for "energy," the capacity to perform a certain amount of work in a certain amount of time. The "m" stands for "mass," the amount of matter in an object. The term "inertia" in Einstein's article refers to the inertia of mass. The greater the inertia of a body, the more energy is required to change it's speed. The "c" stands for the speed of light (ca. 300,000 km/sec). It may be going too far to explain how Einstein derived this formula—so I'll explain its rationale.

The formula indicates that energy and mass are equivalent; they are two sides of the same coin. Mass can be converted into energy and energy can be converted into mass.

| Energy is "liberated" matter, matter is "solidified" energy.

Because c^2 is a huge number, a small amount of mass can be converted into a gigantic amount of energy. At an atomic level, this works as follows: the protons and neutrons in the atomic nucleus have less mass than if they existed separately. This difference in mass is needed to hold these particles together, the so-called strong nuclear force, the strongest of the "four fundamental forces"—well over one hundred times stronger than the electromagnetic force.

The relationship between mass, energy, and speed is illustrated by the following example. Imagine a rocket flying faster and faster, up to about the speed of light. To keep accelerating, this rocket requires more and more energy as the rocket becomes increasingly inert. By the time the rocket reaches the speed of light, its inertia is infinite, and thus an infinite amount of energy is needed to match the speed of light. This leads to the following conclusion.

> No material object can reach the speed of light, which is the speed limit for the universe.[3]

Figure 18. The difference in summation of speeds between Newton and Einstein (c = speed of light, v = any speed).

3. Gregersen, *Britannica Guide to Relativity*, 11.

In Newton's model (appendix 1), it would always be possible to add together the speeds of objects moving in the same direction. According to Einstein, the summation of similarly directed speeds results in a speed that is always smaller than the speed of light.

THE GENERAL THEORY OF RELATIVITY

The "special" thing about the special theory of relativity is that motion is in the absence of gravity or any other force. In the general theory of relativity, gravity comes into play. Einstein had an enormous imagination, and he loved thought experiments. The story goes that one day in 1907, sitting at his desk in the patent office in Bern, he saw a painter at work at the opposite building. And Einstein began to fantasize. Suppose the painter were to fall off the ladder and goes into free fall; would he feel his weight? No, Einstein argued, because he is weightless. This thought led him to the idea of the theory of gravity. Later, Einstein said this had been the happiest thought of his life.

Einstein imagined himself aboard a rocket moving vertically with an acceleration of 9.8 m/sec^2—identical to the acceleration of gravity on earth—in empty space, far from the earth.

Look closely at this drawing, because herein lies the crux of the general theory of relativity!

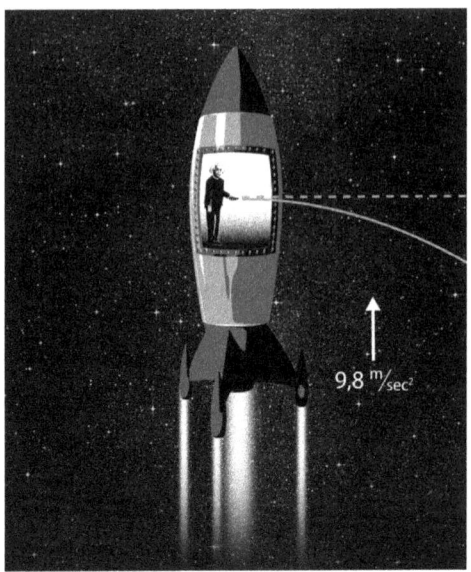

Daniël Maas, 2022
Figure 19. Thought experiment Einstein.

He quickly concluded that it was impossible to distinguish between the effect of gravity on earth and the effect of the rocket's acceleration in empty space; he called this the "equivalence principle." He then wondered what would happen to a ray of light projected onto the wall opposite him, and reasoned that the ray of light would curve downwards due to the fact that, while the ray of light was heading for the wall, the accelerating rocket was moving upwards. In a uniformly moving rocket, the ray of light would have gone in a straight line (dotted) to the wall. Because of the "equivalence principle," this deflection of light should also take place on the earth. But why was the light deflected and not moving in a straight line? Once again, Einstein deduced the right answer: perhaps a curve is the shortest path, just as the shortest path between, say, Amsterdam and New York is curved (a "geodesic"). Perhaps space itself is curved. This can be represented visually as follows:

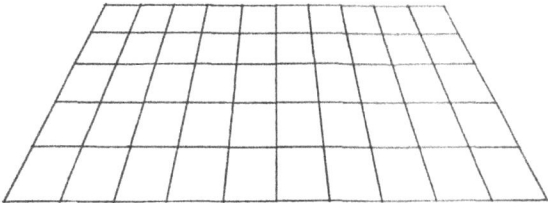

Figure 20. Empty space-time (no influence of matter or energy).

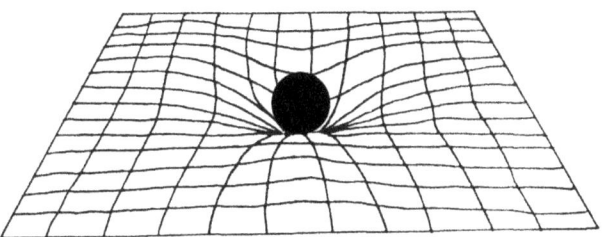

Figure 21. A heavenly body causes a curvature in space-time.

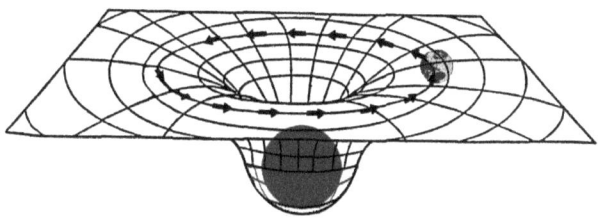

Figure 22. Sun with the earth in an elliptical orbit.

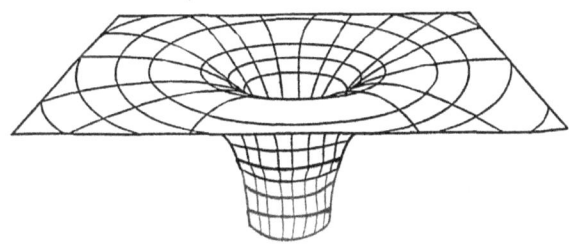

Figure 23. A black hole is an infinitely deep "well" in the fabric of space-time. Or, in mathematical jargon, a discontinuity.

Einstein's conclusion was that the theory of gravity, as devised by Newton, was wrong; there's no force at a distance between two celestial bodies. General relativity teaches us that space and time cannot be considered as two independent entities, as in the world of Isaac Newton. In Einstein's world, space and time are inextricably linked, hence the notion of "space-time." The curvature in the fabric of space-time determines how celestial bodies move:

> Celestial bodies move in principle in a rectilinear fashion but follow the curvature of space-time.

Since light deflects near celestial bodies and does not travel in a straight line, it means that light has to travel a longer distance and hence time is slowed down when near celestial bodies. The greater the mass, the greater the curvature. The greater the curvature, the greater the time delay due to gravity—the gravitational time dilation.

The trampoline figures (figures 20–23) are a simplification of the real situation which consists of three space dimensions and one time dimension, hence a four-dimensional space-time. Unfortunately, it's next to impossible to imagine this four-dimensional space-time; you simply have to rely on the results of the calculations The more curved the space, the slower the clock runs on the spot. In empty space, without the influence of matter or energy, the clock ticks at its fastest. In a black hole, time stands still and the clock no longer ticks.

Imagine if humanity lived on the moon. Because the mass of the moon is much smaller than that of the earth, space-time on the moon is less curved. Therefore, time runs faster on the moon than on planet earth. This means that the average human would age faster on the moon than here on earth. Another example: where do you age faster, on the top floor of an apartment building or on the ground floor? When you go down in an elevator from the top floor to the ground floor, you get closer and closer to the mass of the earth. This means that space-time on the ground floor is more curved than space-time on the top floor. Therefore, time goes faster on the top floor and you will age faster there.

Resuming:

> The greater the mass of a celestial body, the greater the curvature of space-time, the longer the path of light, the slower the time.

The mathematics relating to the four-dimensional space-time coordinate system was so complicated that Einstein, with the help of his then-college friend Hungarian-Swiss mathematician Marcel Grossman (1878–1936), was only able to publish his general theory of relativity eight years later in 1915. The highlight of the general theory of relativity is a mathematical formula—the Einstein equation—describing the curvature of space-time as a function of the presence of matter and energy. Einstein realized that his formula could lead to an imploding universe, and that was not consistent with his intuitive picture of a static universe without a beginning or end. Therefore, in 1917, he adjusted his formula as such by a factor he called the "cosmological constant," which in fact was an "antigravity" force. When measurements by Edwin Hubble, in 1929, showed that the universe indeed expanded, he had to remove the cosmological constant from his formula. He later called this the "biggest blunder" of his life.

The accuracy of Einstein's theory was confirmed by observations and measurements made by British astronomers Sir Frank Dyson (1868–1939) and Sir Arthur Eddington (1882–1944) during the 29 May 1919 solar eclipse. Shortly thereafter, Einstein was asked how he would have reacted if the sun's deflection of light had not been observed: "Then I would have felt sorry for the dear Lord—the theory is correct," Einstein replied.[4] Despite this evidence, a book entitled *100 Authors against Einstein* was published in 1931. Einstein reportedly responded with "to defeat relativity one did not need the word of 100 scientists, but only one fact."[5]

---

4. Parker, *Einstein's Dream*, 43.
5. Gregersen, *Britannica Guide to Relativity*, 57.

Albert Einstein

The American physicist John Wheeler (1911–2008), who coined the term "black hole," summarized the general theory of relativity in one sentence:

> Spacetime tells matter how to move; matter tells spacetime how to curve.[6]

Although Einstein's laws replaced Newton's laws, on earth Newton's laws are still applied when making mechanical calculations. This is because the deviations here on earth are too small to be taken into account. As an example, the world's tallest building—the Burj Khalifa in Dubai—at 829 meters high is still standing there. So a theory in physics doesn't have to be theoretically 100 percent perfect to be applied.

Another example is that of GPS systems. The gravity at the height of the GPS satellites is much lower than here on earth. In addition, they move at a considerable speed relative to the earth. In the first tests with navigation equipment in the early 1990s, the system appeared to work, but every twenty-four hours there was a deviation of eleven kilometers. No one understood why—the software was correct, the maps were correct, and the satellites were working. It took a Dutch engineer to point out the effects of the mathematical equations of Einstein's theory of relativity, which apply when satellites circulate high above the earth. After taking Einstein's equations into account, the navigation systems worked perfectly. So you owe the accuracy of your GPS system to Albert Einstein!

---

6. Wheeler, *Geons*, 235.

Orren Jack Turner, 1947

Albert Einstein (1879–1955)

Albert Einstein is considered the most influential physicist of the twentieth century. As a five-year-old, he was already interested in the fact that a compass needle always points north. As a teenager, he wrote his first paper: "The Investigation of the State of Ether in Magnetic Fields." Ten years later, the same Einstein proved that ether does not exist at all.

After completing his university studies in physics at the Federal Polytechnic Institute in Zurich, Einstein had difficulty finding work, and took a job as a clerk in the patent office in Bern. While there, he developed his special theory of relativity, published in 1905. In the same year, he also devised his famous formula $E = mc^2$ and published a paper in which he launched the notion of an "energy quantum" to explain the photoelectric effect, which later initiated quantum physics. This was his year of glory—he became instantly world-famous. To the general public, Einstein is perhaps best known for his formula $E = mc^2$, which was the stepping-stone to the development of atomic energy and the atomic bomb. Despite being at the cradle of the atomic bomb, he was a staunch pacifist. Einstein was averse to any form of authority, as evidenced by his statement "unthinking respect for authority is the greatest enemy of truth."[7]

In 1933, Einstein fled from Nazi-Germany to America and started working at the renowned Institute for Advanced Study in Princeton, New Jersey, devoting the rest of his life to unifying his theory of relativity and electromagnetism. Einstein was a brilliant, creative thinker and he once said of himself, "I have no special talents, I am only passionately curious."[8] But, he was not the most brilliant mathematician, and he failed to bring both theories under one heading. At the time, he was mostly concerned with world politics and peace issues. In 1952, he was approached by the Israeli government to become President of Israel. However, he declined, saying, "Hence I lack both the natural aptitude and experience to deal properly with people and to exercise official functions."[9]

Was Einstein a religious man? First of all, Einstein was not referring to a religious God. Einstein was born a Jew, but he renounced his faith early on in his life. He explained this in one of his letters, "If something is in me that can be called religious, then it is the unbounded admiration for the structure of the world so far as science can reveal it."[10] In this sense, Einstein's view of God corresponds best to that of the Dutch-Jewish philosopher Baruch Spinoza (1632–1677) as evidenced by Einstein's statement "I believe in Spinoza's God, who reveals himself in the lawful harmony of all that exists, but not in a God who concerns himself with the fates and the doings of mankind."[11]

On 18 April 1955, Einstein was hospitalized with severe aortal problems, but he refused medical intervention. He accepted his fate saying, "I want to go when I want. It is tasteless to prolong life artificially. I have done my share; it's time to go, I will do it elegantly."[12] Albert Einstein died at the age of seventy-six. During

7. Pritscher, *Re-Opening Einstein's Thought*, 13.
8. Marsico, *Genius Physist Albert Einstein*, 30.
9. Bucky and Weakland, *Private Albert Einstein*, 84.
10. Frankenberry, *Faith of Scientists*, 151.
11. Topper, *How Einstein Created Relativity*, 226.
12. Stefan, *Thus Spoke Einstein*, 252.

the autopsy, the pathologist removed Einstein's brain, allegedly without his family's consent, to be used in medical neuroscience training.

One of Albert Einstein's most famous statements reads, "God does not play dice with the universe," or in his own words in German, "Der Alte würfelt nicht."[13] Niels Bohr, one of the founding fathers of quantum physics, reportedly reprimanded Einstein by saying, "Stop telling God what to do."[14] With "der Alte würfelt nicht," Einstein was referring to the new reality of quantum physics that didn't correspond to his harmonious worldview. In 1926, he wrote to his friend Max Born, "Quantum mechanics demands serious attention. But an inner voice tells me that this is still not the true Jacob. The theory accomplishes a lot, but it scarcely brings us closer to the secret of the Old One. In any case, I am convinced that He does not play dice."[15] While both Newton's theory and his own theory of relativity were deterministic in nature, quantum physics is characterized by probabilistic variables. In principle, Einstein had no problem with the application of chance and probabilities in natural science, but he may have hoped that quantum theory would be an interim solution and that a deterministic model would eventually emerge with relatively simple mathematical formulas, as he was used to. With today's knowledge, we know that his wish would not be fulfilled.

13. Cowley, *Why Anything*, 218.
14. Kaku, *Einstein's Cosmos*, 168.
15. Everitt et al., *Quantum Mechanics*, 333.

Appendix 4

Quantum Physics

ONCE AGAIN, I'LL ISSUE a warning! Quantum physics is simply too weird for words. Even more than the theory of relativity, this hocus-pocus physics is completely removed from what you would consider "normal." While, on closer examination, the theory of relativity was somewhat comprehensible, the same really isn't true for quantum physics. The behavior of the very smallest particles can be called downright insane—some examples:

- Particles can be in two or more places at the same time (in classical mechanics, objects can only be in one place at any one time).
- Particles sometimes behave as particles, and sometimes as wave phenomena (objects have only one appearance in classical mechanics).
- When measurements are made on particles they start behaving differently because at quantum level, measurements disturb the state of the particle being measured! (Observations in classical mechanics must be independent of the observer.)

Quantum Physics

Benjamin Couprie, 1927
Figure 24. All the founding fathers of quantum physics gathered in Brussels for the Solvay Conference of 1927.

Nevertheless, quantum physics has now fully proven itself in practice. Thanks to quantum physics, it has been possible to develop several commonly used applications like transistors and integrated circuits, used in computers and televisions. To avoid overstretching your brain, an idea is to think of quantum physics as a thought experiment, because you won't understand it anyway. Quantum physics shows us eminently that human intuition is not suitable for understanding the nature of the very smallest matter. A good metaphor to make quantum physics understandable has yet to be found. And remember, nature does not care at all how we think about it. We should adapt to the laws of nature and not the other way around. Even Einstein cheated by adapting his space-time-curvature formula to his intuition. Anyway, welcome to the world of quantum physics. Get used to it; this is the new reality!

> Those who are not shocked when they first come across quantum theory cannot possibly have understood it.[1]

---

1. Bohr, quoted in Heisenberg, *Physics and Beyond*, 206.

Quantum Physics

I'll start with a brief description of the development of quantum physics, followed by its main characteristics, and finally, I'll give an outline of the major contributors to quantum physics.

Quantum physics is not the work of one person; it has several founding fathers. In 1927, twenty-eight men and one woman gathered for the fifth Solvay Conference in Brussels (figure 24). Ernest Solvay, who financed this conference series, was a Belgian industrialist with a keen interest in physics and chemistry. Albert Einstein, already a celebrity at the time, is in the center of the picture. Quantum physics arose from an attempt to bring matter and light under one heading. Around 1900, the German physicist Max Planck (1858–1947) rejected Newton's classical mechanics theory after finding that energy is not a continuum like flowing water but is emitted in the form of small, discrete packets called quanta (the singular "quantum" means "quantity" in Latin). Contrary to the view of physicists at that time that light was an electromagnetic wave phenomenon, in 1905, Albert Einstein proposed light to be a stream of energy quanta (later called "photons"). Influenced by Einstein, in 1924, French physicist Louis de Broglie (1892–1987) introduced the bright idea that matter-particles (such as electrons) can exhibit wave properties in addition to particle properties, the so-called wave-particle duality. This can best be demonstrated by the so-called "double-slit" experiment, which, as a thought experiment, is a good introduction to the world of quantum physics.

Experiment 1

First of all, we'll use a shotgun to fire lead bullets at a screen in which there are two vertical slits (figure 25). The hail of bullets that passes through the slits then strikes another screen behind it. As would be expected, this results in two vertical lines of impact points.

Quantum Physics

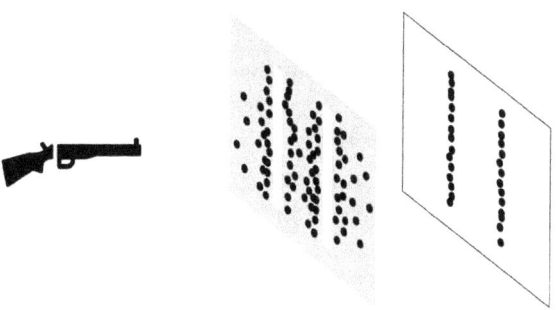

Figure 25. Experiment 1.

Experiment 2

Next, we'll do something similar with water waves in a container (figure 26). If we drop a stone into the water at the location of the black dot, the resulting water waves will move through the two vertical slits in the first screen. This results in two wave fronts behind this screen, which then collide with a second screen, showing a kind of barcode pattern. The white spots in this so-called interference pattern arise at places where the rising wave of one wave front is neutralized by the falling wave of the other wave front, or vice versa. Once again—nothing unusual, this is the expected result.

Figure 26. Experiment 2.

Quantum Physics

Experiment 3

We now enter the quantum world and, using an electron gun, we'll start shooting electrons at a screen with only one vertical slit (figure 27). On the screen behind it, a vertical line of impacted electrons appears, exactly as in experiment 1. The electrons, just like the lead bullets fired from a shotgun in experiment 1, apparently behave like particles.

Figure 27. Experiment 3.

Experiment 4

We'll now shoot electrons at a screen with two vertical slits (figure 28). This time, you might expect another vertical line pattern as shown in experiment 1 but, to our surprise, an *interference pattern* appears on the second screen! Apparently, the electrons are now behaving like waves. Even if we only shoot the electrons one by one, the same interference pattern appears. This means that an electron can simultaneously pass through both slits and in that way, it interferes with itself!

Quantum Physics

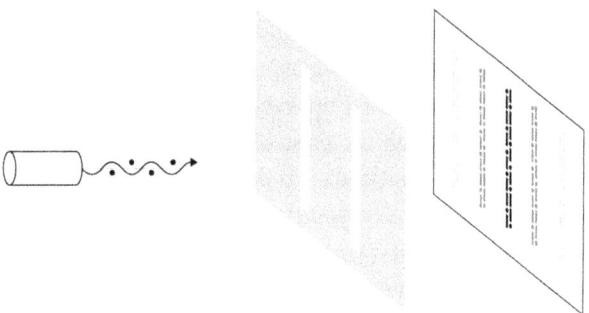

Figure 28. Experiment 4.

Experiment 5

If we now place a detector at the slits to see through which slit the electrons pass (figure 29), to our surprise, a *vertical line pattern* appears on the second screen—not an interference pattern. Apparently, once again, the electrons are behaving like particles! If we then turn off the detector, the second screen again shows the interference pattern. This is bizarre! Electrons behave like waves, but when we look at them, they behave like particles! Obviously, Newton's and Einstein's laws do not apply to this wave-particle phenomenon.

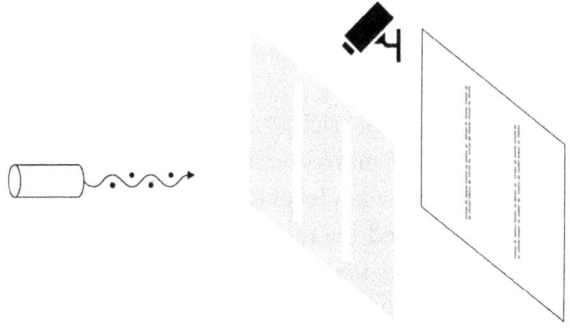

Figure 29. Experiment 5.

Quantum Physics

Another example:

When you look through a window, you can see a faint reflection of your face on the pane—glass is not 100 percent transparent. This can easily be explained by wave theory: the vast majority of light waves pass through the glass so you can see what's going on the other side, but a small part is reflected so you see a faint image of your own face. But . . . if you try to explain this from the point of view of particle theory, you get stuck. After all, why would one photon pass through the glass while the other photon is reflected? All photons are—supposedly—identical! The answer is that in the microworld, although particles are identical, they don't all react identically. This is because for each photon, there's a probability of x percent for it to pass the glass, and a probability of (100-x) percent that it will be reflected. So you can never predict in advance whether a specific photon will pass the glass or not. This probability behavior of elementary particles is a fundamental property of quantum physics.

Danish physicist Niels Bohr (1885–1947) was the first to attempt to describe the structure of atoms using quantum physics. At the time, the view among physicists was that an atom consisted of a positively charged nucleus with a certain mass, with a number of negatively charged electrons floating around it, a kind of microsolar system. In 1923, Bohr published that electrons could only occupy specific orbits around the nucleus based on Planck's constant. When an electron jumps from a higher to a lower orbit, energy is released. For an electron to jump to a higher orbit, energy has to be added.[2]

Shortly after, two physicists, Austrian Erwin Schrödinger (1887–1961) and German Werner Heisenberg (1901–1976), independently developed a model of the atom in which an electron follows an orbital around the nucleus described by a wave function based on probability theory; this is known as the Schrödinger equation. This model contrasted with Bohr's model, in which an electron follows a fixed orbit around the nucleus. Figure 30 shows

---

2. Zettili, *Quantum Mechanics*, 3.

a hydrogen atom according to the Bohr model and according to the Heisenberg-Schrödinger model.

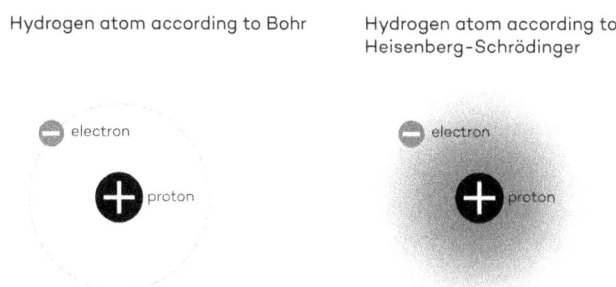

Figure 30. Hydrogen atom according to Bohr and according to Heisenberg-Schrödinger.

Again, the fundamental difference between an orbit and an orbital is the following: an orbit is the circular path that an electron describes during a revolution around the nucleus of an atom; its exact location and speed can be determined at any time. An orbital is a three-dimensional space where there's a significant (95 percent) chance that an electron can be located. An orbital satisfies Heisenberg's uncertainty relation, which implies that you cannot simultaneously determine both the position and the momentum (mass × velocity) of an electron. The more accurate the position of the electron, the more inaccurate its momentum. Or conversely, the more accurate the momentum of the electron, the more inaccurate its position.

Why is Heisenberg's uncertainty relation relevant in the quantum world but not at the macro level?

When you want to measure the state of an electron, you can do so by shining light on it. The smaller the wavelength of that light, the more accurate the measurement result. One or more particles of light (photons) collide with the electron, and the reflected photons then reach your retina or another detector. Since the momentum of a photon is approximately equal to the momentum of an electron, a photon can partially transfer its momentum to the

Quantum Physics

electron upon collision. After the collision, the electron will continue its path at an indefinite speed in an indefinite direction. So you know the exact position where the electron has been hit, but you have no idea where the electron is going at what speed. In other words, at the quantum level, measurement means disruption: the state of the quantum particle to be measured before and after the measurement is not the same. This in effect means that in quantum physics it's not possible to describe the electron's trajectory. Heisenberg's uncertainty principle is the most essential feature of quantum physics. Here is Stephen Hawking's take: "Heisenberg's uncertainty principle is a fundamental, unescapable property of the world."[3] When you shine a ray of light on, say, a billiard ball, the effect of Heisenberg's uncertainty principle is present but negligible because of the gigantic difference in momentum between the photon and the billiard ball. Therefore, the conclusion is that a billiard ball does not exhibit quantum behavior.

Another specific feature is the so-called superposition, the possibility of a particle appearing in two or more places at the same time. The location of a particle is determined by the probability distribution of the wave function according to Schrödinger's formula. Unobserved particles behave like placeless waves. But when the particle's position is measured, as illustrated in the double-slit experiment, something very strange happens: the particle behaves like a particle again and the wave function has suddenly disappeared. In quantum language, the wave function is said to have "collapsed" because the measurement forced the particle, as it were, to make a decision. At that moment, the particle is 100 percent in either one position or 100 percent in another, but no longer in a "superposition."

The concept of superposition opens the door to the quantum computer, a *game changer*. A quantum computer can perform several calculations simultaneously in one step, while a classical computer can only perform one at a time, step by step. A classical computer works with bits (0 *or* 1), whereas a quantum computer works with qubits (0 *and* 1 at the same time). This means that a

---

3. Hawking, *Brief Answers*, 63.

Quantum Physics

quantum computer has exponential computing power over the classical computer's linear computing power. It therefore becomes possible to perform computations that would never have been possible before. The applications for this are already known in practice, first and foremost within the quantum world itself—for example, complex calculations in quantum fields or multidimensional quantum spaces.

> Complex quantum problems can only be solved with a quantum computer.

Furthermore, exciting computational challenges can be found in the fields of materials science and biochemistry. Clearly, IT companies and countries like China and Japan have a massive interest in the quantum computer. However, currently, we expect it to take another ten to twenty years before quantum computers will be available in the public domain. The biggest problem to be solved is to isolate the quantum computer from its environment so that superpositions are maintained.

Another unique property of quantum physics with far-reaching application opportunities is the so-called "entanglement," the phenomenon that pairs of particles can be correlated. Back in 2015, physicists at Delft University of Technology, Netherlands, succeeded in experimentally demonstrating the entanglement of two particles over a distance of 1.3 kilometer. Several years ago, physicists managed to achieve particle entanglement between the La Palma Observatory (Canary Islands) and an observatory on the island of Tenerife: a distance of 150 kilometers.

When particle A on one side is manipulated, particle B on the other side also changes *instantaneously*, even though there is no connection between the two particles at all! In quantum terms: you connect without any existing connection. This means that the transfer from A to B took place at a speed greater than the speed of light! If Albert Einstein could learn of this "spooky action at a distance" he hated, he would rise from his grave and pull all his hairs (and there were a lot of them) out of his head.[4] Physicists have

---

4 Tyson et al., *Welcome to the Universe*, 320.

thus created an absolutely secure connection between two points through this so-called "teleportation." So, if this can be achieved between two points, it must also be achievable between multiple points. This basically opens the way to a hack-free quantum internet.

The Standard Model of Quantum Physics

The standard model is a systematic account of all known elementary particles in quantum physics, similar to the periodic table of elements in chemistry. It explains how certain particles make up all visible matter and how force-carrying particles interact with matter particles.

The model describes three of the four fundamental forces: the electromagnetic force, the strong atomic force and the weak atomic force. Since there is as yet no quantum description of the fourth fundamental force—gravity—this force is not included in the standard model. The challenge here is to unite a probabilistic model (quantum physics) with a deterministic model (Einstein), containing the gravitational force, which is extremely weaker than the other three forces. Still a paradox emerges here: in principle, there is no difference between the matter of the microcosm and that of the macrocosm. Even the very largest celestial bodies consist of the very same particles. And yet somewhere in the theorizing, a short circuit has crept in between these two worlds. Nevertheless, the search for a quantum description of gravity continues unabated.

Currently there are some sixty-one known elementary particles, with exotic names such as quarks, leptons, bosons, fermions, neutrinos, gluons, etc. Of all the elementary particles, perhaps the Higgs particle is best known to the general public. The existence of the Higgs particle was empirically demonstrated in 2012 with the particle accelerator in Geneva, after years earlier British physicist Peter Higgs (1929–present) had predicted the existence of this elementary particle on theoretical grounds. So much for the introduction of the standard model. It would take us, in the context of this book, too far to discuss the standard model in detail.

The Main Founders of Quantum Physics

Given the large number of contributors to the development of quantum physics, it's beyond the scope of this book to give an extensive description of each person and his theory. Therefore, I've limited myself to a brief outline of the main contributors.

Unknown photographer, 1930

Max Planck (1858–1947)

In 1900, Max Planck, a German physicist, distanced himself from classical mechanics and launched the theory that the energy of electromagnetic waves is not a continuous flow, but is emitted in the form of small discrete packets (quanta). This was the beginning of quantum physics. The renowned Max Plank Institute in Germany is named after him.

Ferdinand Schmutzer, 1921

Albert Einstein (1879–1955)

Albert Einstein's theories are described in detail in appendix 3. His contribution to quantum physics consists of a scientific paper (1905) in which he proposed to consider light as a stream of packets of energy (photons). For this paper on the photoelectric effect, he was awarded the 1921 Nobel Prize.

Quantum Physics

Unknown photographer, 1933

Max Born (1882–1970)

Max Born, a Polish-Jewish mathematician and physicist, mainly contributed to quantum physics by his interpretation of the wave nature of elementary particles. He discovered that the square of the maximum wave height (amplitude) is a measure of the probability of encountering a particle at any time at a particular position.

Lagrelius and Westphal, 1922

Niels Bohr (1885–1962)

The Danish physicist Niels Bohr is known as a pioneer of atomic physics. He discovered that electrons could only move in specific orbits determined by the "Planck constant." His profound views on wave-particle duality became known by the term "Copenhagen interpretation."

Quantum Physics

Nobel foundation, 1933

Erwin Schrödinger (1887–1961)

Austrian physicist Erwin Schrödinger is known for the "Schrödinger equation," in which he describes the motions of particles with a mathematical formula based on wave mechanics. More than a physicist, Schrödinger was a renowned womanizer. It's said that, sometime in 1926, he retreated to a mountain hut in the Alps with one of his many mistresses and returned with his famous formula.

Unknown photographer, 1929

Louis de Broglie (1892-1987)

Louis de Broglie was a prominent French physicist, from a distinguished noble family. In 1924, he launched the idea that matter particles (such as electrons) could also exhibit a wave nature. A few years later this was confirmed experimentally, leading to a new branch in physics: wave mechanics.

Unknown photographer, 1940

Wolfgang Pauli (1900–1958)

Wolfgang Pauli, an Austrian-American physicist, made several important contributions to quantum physics but is best known for the exclusion principle named after him. This implies that in an atom, two electrons cannot be in the same quantum state at the same time. He was awarded the Nobel Prize for this in 1945.

Unknown photographer, 1933

Werner Heisenberg (1901–1976)

Werner Heisenberg was a German physicist best known for the uncertainty principle named after him, which implies that one can never know both the position and the momentum of a quantum particle at the same time.

Quantum Physics

Unknown photographer, 1933

Paul Dirac (1902–1984)

Paul Dirac, an English theoretical physicist, is best known for the so-called Dirac equation. This mathematical formula reconciles quantum physics with Albert Einstein's special theory of relativity. On the basis of his formula, Dirac predicted the existence of the hitherto unknown antimatter. This was confirmed experimentally in 1932 with the discovery of the positron, the antiparticle of the electron.

Quantum Physics

Richard Feynman

Well, if you're still baffled by the bizarre world of quantum physics, then you're in good company. Here are the words of one of the most quoted representatives of quantum physics, the eminent and flamboyant Richard Feynman (1918–1988):

> I think I can safely say that nobody understands quantum mechanics.[5]

Unknown photographer

---

5. Everitt et al., *Quantum Mechanics*, 333.

APPENDIX 5

Stephen Hawking

STEPHEN HAWKING WAS APPOINTED professor of physics in 1977 and spent his first few years working on the theory of what was then called "stars collapsed by gravity" or "black holes"—at the time a hot topic. But before we go any further, let's briefly look at what black holes really are.

A black hole occurs when a large star collapses due to its own gravity—its mass must be at least three times the mass of the sun. At some point, all helium in the star's core burns up and the star starts to shrink. At this stage, the star is still visible because light can still escape. But over time, the curvature of space-time (see appendix 3: "Albert Einstein") becomes such that light can no longer escape and the star can therefore no longer be seen with a space telescope. The spherical surface around a black hole within which matter and even light can no longer escape is called the "event horizon." Compare this to Niagara Falls: once you fall over the edge with your canoe, there's no turning back. Finally, the star implodes into a singularity, extremely distorting space-time at the site.

When two galaxies collide, black holes may merge and form a new black hole, which can be many billions of solar masses in size. These collisions between black holes are so violent that they cause ripples in the fabric of space-time, called "gravitational waves" or "Einstein waves." Gravitational waves can be measured by sensitive mirror telescopes, even if these collisions took place billions of light years away from the earth. Using ordinary space telescopes, astronomers can look back in time to a maximum of one hundred million years after the big bang, because no stars existed before then, so no light either; with a mirror telescope, astronomers can measure gravitational waves that originated from shortly after the big bang. In this context, it is interesting to note that currently plans are underway for a new, highly sensitive mirror telescope, possibly to be built on the border between the Netherlands and Belgium.

Black holes can be thought of as the waste pits of the universe. Anything that gets too close, i.e., beyond the event horizon, is irrevocably sucked in. Usually, black holes are located at the center of galaxies. In April 2019, the (virtual) Event Horizon Telescope took the very first picture (figure 31) of a black hole about 55 million light years away from the earth. The mass of this black hole, at the center of galaxy M87, is 6.5 billion times the mass of the sun. In May 2022, using the same Event Horizon Telescope, a picture of another black hole was taken, which was located at the center of our own Milky Way galaxy. Sagittarius A* is 27,000 light years away from the earth and has a mass equal to 4 million times that of the sun, with an event horizon diameter of six million kilometers. The heaviest black hole discovered so far is located at the center of the quasar S5 0014+81, at a distance of 12 billion light years from the earth. The mass of this gigantic monster is estimated at 40 billion solar masses!

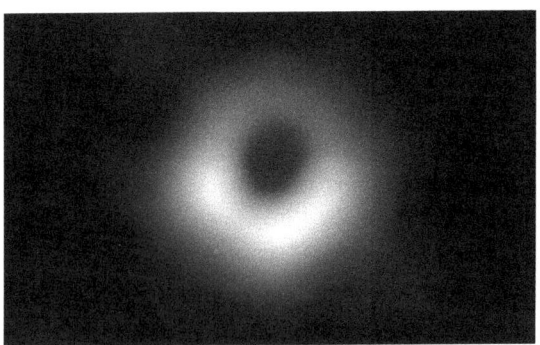

Event Horizon Telescope, 2021
Figure 31. The very first photograph of a black hole.

In the 1970s, the general opinion among physicists was that nothing could escape from a black hole, but Hawking thought otherwise, combining the general theory of relativity with quantum physics to conclude that radiation could indeed escape from a black hole. Due to quantum effects in the event horizon, pairs of virtual particles and antiparticles are constantly being created. When these come back together, the particle ceases to exist. But, Hawking reasoned, it could be possible that one particle is sucked in, while the other escapes in the form of radiation. By emitting this so-called Hawking radiation, a black hole behaves like any other celestial body and has a certain entropy and temperature. As such, a black hole therefore obeys the laws of thermodynamics. By emitting Hawking radiation, a black hole loses mass according to the formula $E = mc^2$. As a result, a black hole will evaporate, although this process is agonizingly slow.

In 1981, after attending a cosmology conference at the Vatican, Hawking renewed his interest in the origin and the end of the universe. In his speech at the Vatican, he introduced a new radical concept for the origin and evolution of the universe, the no-boundary proposal. Hawking: "There ought to be something very special about the boundary conditions of the universe and what can be more special than the condition that there is no boundary?"[1] He compared his no-boundary proposal for the universe to traveling south until you reach the South Pole. From then on, the term "south" loses its meaning. Applied to time before the big bang, the same reasoning leads to the conclusion that the concept of time then expires.

At time $t = 0$ of the big bang, the universe was a singularity and to a singularity Einstein's formulas cannot be applied because they lead to infinite outcomes. Isn't it curious that Einstein's space-time-curvature formula breaks down right at the start at $t = 0$? On this, Hawking said the following: "Thus classical general relativity brings about its own downfall: it predicts that it can't predict the universe. Although many people welcomed this conclusion, it has always profoundly disturbed me. If the laws of physics could break

---

1. Drees, *Beyond the Big Bang*, 235.

down at the beginning of the universe, why couldn't they break down anywhere?"² So Hawking was looking for a solution to get rid of the big bang singularity, while he himself had proven in 1965 that an expanding universe must have started with a singularity in the first place. But also the laws of quantum theory cannot be applied to the big bang singularity because the underlying mass is infinitely large. Therefore, Hartle and Hawking devised a mathematical trick by introducing the concept of imaginary time into their model. Indeed, unlike real time, imaginary time does hold at a singularity.

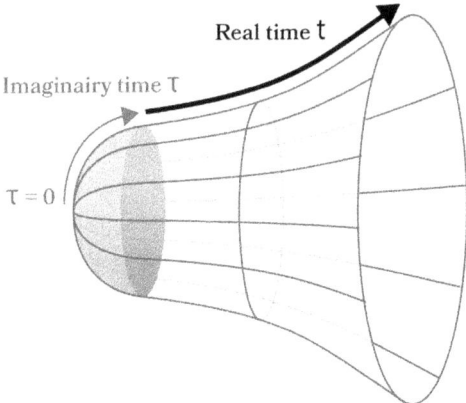

Figure 32. The Hartle–Hawking model

Hartle and Hawking arrived at a model of the universe whose shape resembles a badminton shuttle. Just as a badminton shuttle has no starting point at the bottom (mathematically, on the spot, the diameter equals zero) and gets wider and wider from there, the Hartle–Hawking model also has no starting point.

| The no-boundary proposal has no big bang singularity!

Hartle and Hawking worked out a formula for the entire shuttle shape, the so-called wave function of the universe that describes the past, present, and future as one. The Hartle–Hawking

---

2. Hawking and Penrose, *Nature of Space and Time*, 75–76.

model is self-contained which means that it has no starting conditions and no starting point. Hawking says about this, "So long as the universe had a beginning, we could suppose it had a creator. But if the universe is really completely self-contained, having no boundary or edge, it would have neither have a beginning, nor end: it would simply be. What place, then, for a creator?"[3] The no-boundary proposal is above all a brilliant thought experiment by two creative minds. Obviously, it is a theoretical model, which has not been empirically tested yet.

In his later life, Hawking mainly worked on the unification of the general theory of relativity and quantum physics. The most promising candidate for a solution is the so-called "string theory." This theory assumes that all elementary particles in the universe are not point particles, but micro-elastics that can vibrate in all sorts of ways, called "strings." A good metaphor for string theory is a violin, as a violin string can produce many sounds. High, low, sharp, warm, it depends on how a musician decides to use bow and fingers to touch a string—yet it remains just one string. In other words, in this theory, the way a string "vibrates" determines whether it is an electron, or a meson, or a muon, etc. Hence, the choice of the term "string."

If string theory succeeds in providing a quantum description of gravity, then the holy grail of unifying the four fundamental forces—the "theory of everything"—is within reach. However, there are still many problems integrating the other fundamental forces into the string theory. The current version of the string model assumes that the microworld consists of ten dimensions—six dimensions more than Einstein's space-time model. The latest development in this field is that five existing ten-dimensional string theories are being integrated into one overarching eleven-dimensional superstring theory, the so-called M-theory. It's my impression that string theory, as the best candidate for the "theory of everything," is currently losing momentum.

With the current generation of particle accelerators, it is not possible to make measurements in these dimensions. So, even if the theory is mathematically consistent, we cannot directly test this

---

3. Hawking, *Brief History of Time*, 160–61.

theory experimentally. For now, a consistent mathematical theory has yet to be found. However, American physicist Brian Greene (1963–present), world-renowned for his pioneering discoveries in string theory, is optimistic: "String theory is the most developed theory with the capacity to unite general relativity and quantum mechanics in a consistent manner. I do believe the universe is consistent, and therefore I do believe that general relativity and quantum mechanics should be put together in a manner that makes sense."[4]

DWDD, 2018
Prof. Thomas Hertog

Together with Belgian cosmologist and theoretical physicist Thomas Hertog (1975–present), Hawking worked on a new version of the big bang theory for some twenty years, until just before his death. The driver for his new way of thinking was the fact that Hawking became increasingly puzzled about the bio-friendly character of our universe.

Their main conclusion was that the big bang is the origin of time and that the laws of nature were not preset, but evolved simultaneously with the big bang. Hawking and Hertog applied quantum theory to the big bang, similar to the quantum theory of black holes, developed by Hawking in the 1970s. They also drew a parallel with Darwin's theory of evolution, in which the development of life and time also evolved together. Except, the development

---

4. McLeish and Hitchings, *Let There Be Science*, 102.

of life covered a period of billions of years, while the evolution of natural laws took place mainly in the inflationary period of the big bang, which occurred in a tiny fraction of a second. Their theory was made public in April 2018, just after Hawking's death, in the *Journal of High Energy Physics* in an article called "A Smooth Exit from Eternal Inflation."[5] The authors herein argue that the prevailing theory of eternal cosmic inflation is incorrect. They therefore reject a multiverse with infinitely many different universes and describe a model with a limited number of universes. Based on holographic quantum cosmology, Hawking and Hertog showed that nothing existed before the big bang. Thomas Hertog: "In all my equations, the other side—or before the big bang as you would say—is just simply not there. There's no notion of time."[6] Hawking and Hertog's new big bang theory could possibly be tested if, in future, with even more advanced mirror telescopes than currently available, physicists would be able to detect the gravitational waves of the big bang itself.

5. Hawking and Hertog, "Smooth Exit from Eternal Inflation?"
6. Hertog, "I Opened a Bottle," para. 15.

NASA, 1999

Stephen Hawking (1942–2018)

As a child, Stephen Hawking was fascinated with physics and the night sky. He initially wanted to study mathematics, but it eventually became physics and cosmology. In 1962, at the age of twenty, he graduated with honors and went on to earn a PhD in cosmology at Cambridge University. In his thesis "Properties of Expanding Universes," he showed that from general theory of relativity it follows that the expanding universe must have started with a singularity: the big bang singularity. In 1979, he became Lucasian Professor of Mathematics, a chair that Isaac Newton had also held.

After his diagnosis of ALS at the age of twenty-one, doctors predicted that he only had two years to live. Initially, he lapsed into severe depression, but after some time he picked up where he left off. Shortly after his diagnosis, he fell down from a stone staircase in Cambridge. He had hurt himself in the process to the extent that he was worried he had suffered brain damage, so he asked for an intelligence test. After hearing the results, he was able to continue his academic work with confidence—his IQ was found to be somewhere between 200 and 250.

Hawking wrote fifteen books. The most famous one, *A Brief History of Time*, has sold twenty million copies. He wrote his books to generate income for his family. As early as 1969, his career had boomed—although his progressive illness forced him to use a wheelchair. In 1974, a few weeks after the publication of his paper on black holes, Hawking received Britain's highest academic award; at the age of thirty-two, he was admitted to the prestigious Royal Society. In 1985, aged forty-two, he permanently lost his voice and required twenty-four-hour nursing care. At the time, an American programmer had developed a speech program based on head and eye movements. This allowed Hawking to continue his productive work. In 2007, he visited Kennedy Space Center in Florida and made a flight in a modified Boeing 727, in which he was able to experience weightlessness. Hawking's weightless flight was his greatest wish. For a while, he was able to forget about his paralyzed body; these were moments of true happiness.

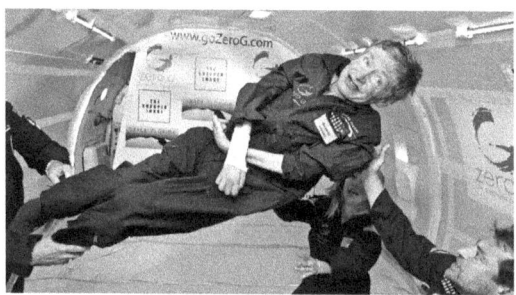

Jim Campbell, 2007
Figure 33. The weightless Hawking.

Hawking was known for his unconventional statements, not only about his field of expertise, but also about politics, climate, and other threats to our planet. He made regular appearances on television shows worldwide and played himself in an episode of the television series *The Big Bang Theory*. In 2014, the film *The Theory of Everything* about life with his first wife Jane Wilde was released. Hawking enjoyed practical jokes—he once organized a party to which only time travelers were invited. He sent out the invitations after the party so that only time travelers could have found the venue in time. Of course, no one showed up.

Did Hawking believe in God? Let him speak for himself: "We are each free to believe what we want and it is my view that the simplest explanation is there is no God. No one created the universe, and no one directs our fate. This leads me to a profound realization. There is probably no heaven, and no afterlife either. I think belief in an afterlife is just wishful thinking . . . We have this one life to appreciate the grand design of the universe, and for that I am extremely grateful."[7]

Stephen Hawking died of ALS at his home in Cambridge on 14 March 2018, more than fifty years later than his doctors had predicted. He, like Albert Einstein, had hoped to see the "theory of everything" come to fruition during his lifetime, but sadly this was not to be. The ashes of his body are interred in Westminster Abbey, where Isaac Newton and Charles Darwin are also to be found.

---

7. Hawking, *Brief Answers*, 38.

Glossary

Please note: bold terms in the descriptions below also appear as items in the list.

Abiogenesis—Evolutionary process by which living organisms arise from simple organic compounds such as amino acids.

Abrahamic religions—Judaism, Christianity, and Islam.

Acceleration—The extent to which the speed of an object increases within a given unit of time.

Afterlife—For Jews, this is heaven or hell, for Christians it is heaven, hell, or purgatory, and for Muslims it is paradise or hell.

Agnostic—Someone who believes that you cannot know whether God exists.

Atheist—Someone who denies the existence of God.

Atom (Greek: indivisible)—The structure of all chemical elements, consisting of a **nucleus** comprising **protons** and **neutrons** with **electrons** moving at a distance from the nucleus.

Big bang—Beginning of the **universe**, of **matter** and **energy**, of space and time.

Big bang singularity—The state (**singularity**) the **universe** was in at time t = 0 of the **big bang**.

Black hole—**Singularity** in **space-time**, formed by a collapsed star. Even light, having passed the **event horizon**, cannot escape, hence the term "black hole."

Glossary

Constants of nature—Fixed values in physical formulas; for example, **Planck's constant**, the **speed of light**, and the **gravitational constant**. Some constants of nature, such as the fine structure constant, are dimensionless and are called fundamental constants of nature.

Cosmic background radiation—Microwave radiation from the extremely hot phase of the **big bang**—380.000 years after time t = 0—which is still present everywhere in the **universe**. This cosmic radiation enabled cosmologists to create a "baby picture" of the early universe.

Cosmic calendar—Way of putting time in perspective by projecting a long span of time onto a period of one year.

Cosmological constant—Additional factor in the **Einstein equation** to create a static **universe**.

Cosmos—Synonym for the **universe**. Cosmos means order in Greek, which is opposed to chaos, meaning disorder.

Creationist—Person who attributes the origin and development of the **universe** and life to a creator, religious or otherwise.

Dark energy—**Energy** in the **universe** that cannot be observed directly, but which is responsible for the expansion of the universe. An estimated 68 percent of the universe consists of dark energy.

Dark matter—**Matter** in the **universe** that cannot be observed directly but, based on gravity calculations, has to be present. An estimated 85 percent of all matter in the universe consists of dark matter.

Einstein waves—See **gravitational waves**.

Einstein equation—Mathematical formula describing the curvature of **space-time** as a function of the presence of **matter** and **energy**.

Elementary particle—Particle that can no longer be broken down into other particles; e.g., **electrons** and **quarks**.

Glossary

Electron—Negatively charged **elementary particle** of an **atom**, moving at a distance from the **nucleus**.

Energy—The capacity of a physical system to perform a certain amount of work in a certain amount of time.

Entanglement—Phenomenon that two **quantum particles** are correlated to each other. When one particle changes, the other one changes instantaneously, regardless of their distance apart.

Entropy—Thermodynamic concept that describes the degree of disorder in a system. Entropy can only remain the same or increase over time, but can never decrease.

Eukaryotes (Greek: true nucleus)—Complex cells consisting of a nucleus in which RNA/DNA is stored, as well as a number of organelles (mini-organs), usually surrounded by a membrane. The precursors of eukaryotes were the relatively simple "prokaryotes," which had no nucleus.

Event horizon—Spherical surface around a **black hole** within which nothing can escape, including light.

Evolution Theory (Darwin)—Theory on the origin of species by **natural selection**.

Fine-tuning argument—Discovery within cosmology that if the values of the **constants of nature** deviate even a fraction from current values, atoms, stars, planets and (human) life could not exist.

The **first law of thermodynamics**—Law of nature, stating that **energy** can neither be created nor destroyed. Energy can only be transformed into another form. This law is also known as the law of conservation of energy.

The **four fundamental forces**—The gravitational force, the electromagnetic force, the strong nuclear force, and the weak nuclear force.

Glossary

Frequency—The number of complete wave cycles (periods) per unit of time, usually expressed in hertz (one hertz is one period per second).

General theory of relativity—Description of the curvature of **space-time** due to the presence of **matter** and **energy**.

Geodesic curve—The shortest distance between two points in curved space.

God—A creator, religious or otherwise.

God-of-the-gaps—Introducing God to explain the mysteries in the creation story that cannot (yet) be explained by natural science.

Gravity—Attraction between two or more (celestial) bodies, at least according to Isaac Newton's theory. Albert Einstein, on the other hand, claims that Newton's alleged attraction does not exist and that the motions of (celestial) bodies are dictated by the curvature of **space-time**.

Gravitational constant—**Constant of nature** in Newton's law of gravitation.

Gravitational waves—Ripples in the fabric of **space-time** caused by the **big bang** or by orbiting and colliding **black holes**.

Gravity-related time dilation—Time dilation that occurs as a result of the curvature of **space-time** due to the presence of **matter** or **energy**. See also **motion-related time dilation**.

Heisenberg's uncertainty principle—also known as Heisenberg's indeterminacy principle, which implies that you cannot simultaneously know both the position and the momentum (mass × velocity) of a **quantum particle**. The more accurate the measurement of the position, the more inaccurate the measurement of the momentum, or vice versa.

Imaginary time—Time expressed as a number whose square can be negative. According to Stephen Hawking, imaginary time is not imaginary in the sense of unreal, but is just a mathematical term that can be calculated with.

Glossary

Intelligent design—Movement whose adherents claim that the complexity of the **cosmos** and life can only be explained by the existence of an intelligent designer.

Interference—The resulting wave motion when several waves interact. In some places the waves amplify each other, in others they cancel each other out.

Light year—The distance light travels in one year, i.e., 9.46 trillion kilometers.

Mass—The amount of **matter** in an object. The greater the mass, the greater its resistance to **acceleration** (inertia).

Matter—Something that occupies a certain space and has a certain **mass**. An estimated 5 percent of the universe consists of visual matter.

Metaphysics—Doctrine of supernatural phenomena.

Momentum—Measure for **mass** in motion (mass × velocity).

Motion-related time dilation—Phenomenon that from the perspective of an observer in steady straight-line motion or at rest, time of fast moving objects slows down. See also **gravity-related time dilation**.

M-theory—Unification of five known ten-dimensional **string theories** into one overarching eleven-dimensional superstring theory.

Multiverse theory—Theory, arising from **quantum physics**, that many other, if not infinitely many, parallel universes exist in addition to our **universe**.

Natural science—Umbrella term for sciences that study the nature and workings of natural phenomena, including physics, chemistry, and biology with mathematics as a tool for deriving and describing the laws of nature.

Naturalist—Person who holds the view that the origin and development of the **universe** and life can be explained purely by **natural science**, and not by the intervention of a creator.

Glossary

Natural selection—Term from Darwin's **evolutionary theory** referring to the phenomenon that organisms within a population that are best adapted to their environment or to changing conditions have the best chances of survival.

Neutron—Uncharged particle in the atomic **nucleus**.

No-boundary proposal—Quantum theory on the origin of the **universe** developed by Stephen Hawking and James Hartle, in which the **big bang singularity** is eliminated.

Nuclear fusion—Process by which two or more atomic nuclei fuse into one atomic **nucleus**.

Nucleus—The core of an **atom**, consisting of **protons** and **neutrons**, held together by the strong nuclear force.

Particle accelerator—A facility in which **elementary particles** are accelerated by electromagnetic fields to almost the **speed of light** and then allowed to collide in a controlled manner. The world's largest particle accelerator, the CERN organization's Large Hadron Collider, is located near Geneva in Switzerland. The underground tunnel in which the LHC is positioned has a circular circumference of about 27 kilometers, and on average is about one hundred meters underground.

Planck constant—Factor in all **quantum physics** formulas indicating the ratio between the **energy** and **frequency** of a quantum of light (photon).

Positron—Positively charged antiparticle of the **electron**.

Proton—Positively charged particle in the atomic **nucleus**.

Quantum (Latin: quantity)—Smallest possible quantity of, for example, **matter**, **energy**, light, or time.

Quantum fluctuations—Temporal changes in energy levels in empty space in which virtual particles and antiparticles appear and disappear, in accordance with Einstein's formula $E = mc^2$.

Quantum particle—See **elementary particle**.

Glossary

Quantum physics—Scientific theory about the nature and behavior of the very smallest particles.

Quarks—**Elementary particles** that constitute **protons** and **neutrons**.

Quasar—An extremely luminous center of a galaxy from the early days of the **universe**, located billions of **light years** away from the earth.

Scholastics—The prevailing church intelligentsia in the late Middle Ages. Well-known scholastics include Anselm of Canterbury and Thomas Aquinas.

Scientific method (in physics)—Testing whether the predicted observations of a new theory are confirmed or falsified.

The **second law of thermodynamics**—Law of nature stating that the **entropy** (degree of disorder) in a closed system remains the same or increases with the passage of time. Entropy can never decrease.

Singularity—A point of infinitesimal volume and infinite **mass**. In a singularity the laws of nature are no longer valid.

Space-time—Four-dimensional model integrating three-dimensional space and time. It follows from the **general theory of relativity** that space and time cannot be considered separately.

Special theory of relativity—Theory about space and time of observers and objects in steady straight-line motion or at rest, based on the premise that the speed of light is always and everywhere the same, i.e., independent of the speed of the light source.

Speed of light—The speed at which light propagates. In vacuum, this is about 300,000 km/sec.

The **spirit**—In this book, the spirit is completely arbitrarily referred to as the incorporeal part of man that goes to the **afterlife**.

Glossary

The **standard model of quantum physics**—Systematic survey of all known matter particles and force-bearing particles of three fundamental forces, namely the electromagnetic force, the strong atomic force, and the weak atomic force. The model currently counts sixty-one **elementary particles**, but it is not yet complete. In particular, **gravity** is still missing.

String theory—Quantum description of waves on one-dimensional strings. String theory is one of the candidates for the **theory of everything**.

Superposition—Phenomenon that **quantum particles** can be in two different states (particle and wave) at the same time or in two or more places at the same time, regardless of the distance between them.

Syllogistics—Formal logical reasoning based on two premises, one specific and one general, from which a conclusion then follows. This mode of reasoning was commonly used at the time of Aristotle and has lost none of its value.

Teleportation—Phenomenon from **quantum physics** that a **quantum particle** can be "moved" instantaneously over a (large) distance.

Theory of everything—Quantum description of a model integrating the **four fundamental forces**. Physicists are still searching for this holy grail.

Unification theory—Quantum theory of two or more of the **four fundamental forces**.

Universe—All of **space-time** and its contents of **matter** and **energy**.

Wavelength—The distance between two successive peaks or troughs of a wave.

Wave-particle duality—Phenomenon from **quantum physics** that **elementary particles** sometimes behave like particles, and sometimes like waves.

Sources of Illustrations

Chapter 1: Proof of God

2 Figure 1: https://commons.wikimedia.org/wiki/Category:Illustrations_of_Moses#/media/File:Foster_Bible_Pictures_0009-1.jpg
4 Anselm of Canterbury: https://commons.wikimedia.org/wiki/File:Anselm_of_Canterbury.jpg.
5 Thomas Aquinas: https://commons.wikimedia.org/wiki/File:Saint_Thomas_Aquinas_(Crivelli,_15th-century).jpg.
6 René Descartes: https://commons.wikimedia.org/wiki/File:Frans_Hals_-_Portret_van_Ren%C3%A9_Descartes.jpg.
7 Baruch Spinoza: https://commons.wikimedia.org/wiki/File:Spinoza.jpg.

Chapter 2: A Quick Look at Religion

12 Nicolaus Copernicus: https://commons.wikimedia.org/wiki/File:Nicolaus_Copernicus._Reproduction_of_line_engraving.jpg.
13 Charles Darwin: https://commons.wikimedia.org/wiki/File:Charles_Darwin_01.jpg.
14 Gregor Mendel: https://commons.wikimedia.org/wiki/File:Gregor_Mendel.png.
15 Geoges Lemaître: https://commons.wikimedia.org/wiki/File:Lemaitre.jpg.
17 Figure 2: https://commons.wikimedia.org/wiki/File:Rashid_al-Din_Tabib_-_Jami_al-Tawarikh,_f.45v_detail_-_c._1306–15.png.

SOURCES OF ILLUSTRATIONS

Chapter 3: Considering Philosophy

26   René Descartes: https://commons.wikimedia.org/w/index.php?title=Specia l:Search&limit=20&offset=20&ns0=1&ns6=1&ns12=1&ns14=1&ns100=1 &ns106=1&search=Ren%C3%A9+Descartes#/media/File:Descartes3.jpg.

Chapter 4: And Then There Was Life

32   Figure 3: https://commons.wikimedia.org/wiki/File:CMB_Timeline 300_no_WMAP.jpg.
36   Figure 4: https://commons.wikimedia.org/wiki/File:Tiktaalik_roseae_ life_restor.jpg.
37   Figure 5: https://commons.wikimedia.org/wiki/File:T._H._Huxley,_ Evidence_as_to_man%27s_place_in_nature._Wellcome_L0027093.jpg.

Chapter 7: The Body-Spirit Issue

47   Plato: https://commons.wikimedia.org/wiki/File:Plato_Pio-Clemetino _Inv305.jpg.
48   Aristotle: https://commons.wikimedia.org/wiki/File:Aristotle_Altemps_ Inv8575.jpg.
49   Thomas Hobbes: https://commons.wikimedia.org/wiki/File:Thomas_ Hobbes_(portrait).jpg.
50   René Descartes: https://commons.wikimedia.org/wiki/File:Frans_ Hals_-_Portret_van_Ren%C3%A9_Descartes_(cropped)3.jpg.
51   Duncan MacDougall: https://commons.wikimedia.org/wiki/ File:Duncan_MacDougall_physician.png.

Chapter 10: The Future of the Universe

73   Figure 8: https://www.alamy.com/stock-photo-multiple-glowing-bubble -universes-fractal-computer-generated-abstract-173326853.html.

Appendix 1: Isaac Newton

80   Figure 9: https://commons.wikimedia.org/wiki/File:Newton_portrait_ with_apple_tree.svg.
80   Figure 10: https://commons.wikimedia.org/wiki/File:Newton-Principia -Mathematica_1-500x700.jpg.

Sources of Illustrations

83   Isaac Newton: https://commons.wikimedia.org/wiki/File:Sir_Isaac_Newton_(1643-1727).jpg

Appendix 2: Charles Darwin

86   Figure 12: https://commons.wikimedia.org/wiki/File:Man_is_But_a_Worm.jpg

87   Figure 13: https://commons.wikimedia.org/wiki/File:Mutation_and_selection_diagram_NL.svg#/media/File:Mutation_and_selection_diagram.svg

89   Charles Darwin: https://commons.wikimedia.org/wiki/File:Charles_Robert_Darwin,_aged_40._Lithograph_by_T._H._Maguire,_Wellcome_V0001461_(cropped).jpg.

90   Figure 14: https://commons.wikimedia.org/wiki/File:Es-Darwin%27s_finches.jpeg.

Appendix 3: Albert Einstein

96   Figure 16: https://commons.wikimedia.org/wiki/File:Lemaitre.jpg#/media/File:MillikanLemaitreEinstein.jpg.

97   Figure 17 is a combination of https://commons.wikimedia.org/wiki/Category:Portrait_photographs_of_Albert_Einstein#/media/File:Einstein_Blackboard_Exploitable_template.jpg and free stock photo https://stock.adobe.com/be_nl/images/albert-einstein-e-mc2-physical-formula-on-blackboard/10611306.

105   Albert Einstein: https://commons.wikimedia.org/wiki/File:Albert_Einstein_Head.jpg.

Appendix 4: Quantum Physics

109   Figure 24: https://commons.wikimedia.org/wiki/File:Solvay_conference_1927_restored.jpg.

119   Max Planck: https://commons.wikimedia.org/wiki/File:Max_Planck_(1858–1947).jpg.

120   Albert Einstein: https://commons.wikimedia.org/wiki/File:Einstein1921_by_F_Schmutzer_4.jpg.

121   Max Born: https://commons.wikimedia.org/wiki/File:Max_Born.jpg.

122   Niels Bohr: https://commons.wikimedia.org/wiki/File:Niels_Bohr.jpg.

123   Erwin Schrödinger: https://commons.wikimedia.org/wiki/File:Erwin_Schr%C3%B6dinger_(1933).jpg.

Sources of Illustrations

124 Louis de Broglie: https://commons.wikimedia.org/wiki/File:Broglie_Big.jpg.
125 Wolfgang Pauli: https://commons.wikimedia.org/wiki/File:Wolfgang_Pauli_(1900%E2%80%931958),_Austrian_physicist.jpg.
126 Werner Heisenberg: https://commons.wikimedia.org/wiki/File:Bundesarchiv_Bild183-R57262,_Werner_Heisenberg.jpg.
127 Paul Dirac: https://commons.wikimedia.org/wiki/File:Paul_Dirac,_1933.jpg.
128 Richard Feynman: https://commons.wikimedia.org/wiki/File:Richard_Feynman_1988.png.

Appendix 5: Stephen Hawking

130 Figure 31: https://commons.wikimedia.org/wiki/File:A_view_of_the_M87_supermassive_black_hole_in_polarised_light.tif.
134 Prof. Thomas Hertog: https://commons.wikimedia.org/wiki/File:Thomas_Hertog_(2018).jpg.
136 Stephen Hawking: https://commons.wikimedia.org/wiki/File:Stephen_Hawking.StarChild_colorized.jpg.
137 Figure 33: https://commons.wikimedia.org/wiki/File:Physicist_Stephen_Hawking_in_Zero_Gravity_NASA.jpg.

Bibliography

"Age of the Universe." Wikipedia, last edited Apr 15, 2024. https://en.wikipedia.org/wiki/Age_of_the_universe.

Ali, Maulana M. *The Koran (Al-Qur'an): Arabic-English Bilingual Edition with an Introduction of Mohamed A. 'Arafa.* Hinsdale, IL: Time/Teller, 2018.

Akre, Karin, and John P. Rafferty. "Miller-Urey Experiment." Last edited Dec 19, 2023. https://www.britannica.com/science/Miller-Urey-experiment.

Baird, Christopher S. "Where Is the Edge of the Universe?" Science Answering Questions with Surprising Answers, Jan 20, 2016. https://www.wtamu.edu/~cbaird/sq/2016/01/20/where-is-the-edge-of-the-universe/.

Battersby, Stephen. "Eight Extremes: The Densest Thing in the Universe." NewScientist, Mar 2, 2011. https://www.newscientist.com/article/mg20928026-900-eight-extremes-the-densest-thing-in-the-universe/.

Betz, Eric. "Where Is the Edge of the Universe?" Astronomy, Aug 31, 2023. https://www.astronomy.com/science/where-is-the-edge-of-the-universe/.

"Big Bang Nucleosynthesis." Wikipedia, last edited Apr 11, 2024. https://en.wikipedia.org/wiki/Big_Bang_nucleosynthesis.

"Big Crunch." Wikipedia, last edited Apr 27, 2024. https://en.wikipedia.org/wiki/Big_Crunch.

Bishop, Paul, ed. *A Companion to Friedrich Nietzsche: Life and Works.* Rochester, NY: Vintage, 2012.

Bromiley, Geoffrey W. *Historical Theology: An Introduction.* Edinburgh, Scotland: T&T Clark, 2002.

Brown, William, and Andrew C. Fabian. *Darwin.* Cambridge: Cambridge University Press, 2010.

Bucky, Peter A., and Allen G. Weakland. *The Private Albert Einstein.* Kansas City: Andrews and McMeel, 2010.

Castelvecchi, Davide. "Universe Has Ten Times More Galaxies than Researchers Thought." Nature, Oct 14, 2016. https://www.nature.com/articles/nature.2016.20809.

"Chicxulub: The Asteroid That Killed the Dinosaurs." NewScientist, n.d. https://www.newscientist.com/definition/chicxulub/.

Bibliography

Choi, Charles Q. "Earth's Sun: Facts about the Sun's Age, Size and History." Space, Mar 23, 2022. https://www.space.com/58-the-sun-formation-facts-and-characteristics.html.

Connelly, James. *Wittgenstein Early Analytic Semantics: Toward a Phenomenology of Truth*. Lanham, MD: Lexington, 2015.

Copernicus, Nicolaus. *On the Revolutions of the Heavenly Spheres*. Concise ed. Translated by Marika Taylor. London: Flame Tree, 2024.

Cowley, Captain Robert. *Why Anything, Why Not Nothing: The Goldilocks Paragon*. Raleigh, NC: Lulu, 2019.

Craig, William Lane. *The Cosmological Argument from Plato to Leibniz*. Eugene, OR: Wipf & Stock, 2021.

Darwin, Charles. Charles Darwin to John Fordyce, May 7, 1879. In *The Darwin Correspondence Project*, no. 12041. Cambridge: University of Cambridge.

Dascal, Marcelo. *Leibniz: What Kind of Rationalist?* Dordrecht, The Netherlands: Springer, 2008.

Debrock, G., and Paul B. Schreurer, eds. *Newton's Scientific and Philosophical Legacy*. Dordrecht, Netherlands: Kluwer Academic, 1988.

Descartes, René. *Discourse on Method and Meditations on First Philosophy*. 4th ed. Translated by Donald A. Cress. Indianapolis: Hacket, 1998.

———. *Principles of Philosophy*. Whithorn, UK: Anodos, 2017.

"Discovery Boosts Theory That Life on Earth Arose from RNA-DNA Mix." Scripps Research, Dec 23, 2020. https://www.scripps.edu/news-and-events/press-room/2020/20201223-krishnamurthy-dna.html.

Drake, Nadia. "Our Galaxy Is Due to Crash into Its Neighbor—but When?" National Geographic, Feb 9, 2019. https://www.nationalgeographic.co.uk/space/2019/02/our-galaxy-is-due-to-crash-into-its-neighbor-but-when.

Drees, Willem B. *Beyond the Big Bang: Quantum Cosmologies and God*. Peru, IL: Open Court, 1990.

"Earliest Known Life Forms." Wikipedia, last edited Mar 19, 2024. https://en.wikipedia.org/wiki/Earliest_known_life_forms.

"The Early Universe." CERN, n.d. https://home.cern/science/physics/early-universe.

Evergreen, Brian. *Autonomous Transformation: Creating a More Human Future in the Era of Artificial Intelligence*. Hoboken, NJ: Wiley, 2023.

Everitt, Bjergstrom, et al. *Quantum Mechanics*. Hoboken, NJ: Wiley, 2023.

Ferguson, Kitty. *Stephen Hawking: A Life Well Lived*. London: Transworld, 2011.

Ford, Kenneth W. *The Quantum World: Quantum Physics for Everyone*. Cambridge, MA: Harvard University Press, 2009.

Frankenberry, Nancy K., ed. *The Faith of Scientists: In Their Own Words*. Princeton: Princeton University Press, 2008.

"Future of an Expanding Universe." Wikipedia, last edited Mar 31, 2024. https://en.wikipedia.org/wiki/Future_of_an_expanding_universe.

Gregersen, Erik. *Britannica Guide to Relativity and Quantum Mechanics*. New York: Britannica Educational, 2011.

Bibliography

Guth, Alan H., and David I. Kaiser. "Inflationary Cosmology: Exploring the Universe from the Smallest to the Largest Scales." Science 307 (2005) 884-90. https://ned.ipac.caltech.edu/level5/March05/Guth/Guth_contents.html.

Hallam, Henry. *Introduction to the Literature of Europe in the 15th, 16th, and 17th Centuries.* Vol. 2. New York: Harper & Brothers, 1847. https://www.google.es/books/edition/Introduction_to_the_Literature_of_Europe/jewIAAAAQAAJ?hl=nl&gbpv=0.

Hawking, Stephen. *Brief Answers to the Big Questions.* London: John Murray, 2018.

———. *A Brief History of Time.* Updated Bantam ed. London: Penguin Random House, 2016.

Hawking, Stephen, and Roger Penrose. *The Nature of Space and Time.* Princeton: Princeton University Press, 2000.

Hawking, Stephen, and Thomas Hertog. "A Smooth Exit from Eternal Inflation?" *Journal of High Energy Physics* 147 (April 2018).

Heisenberg, Werner. *Physics and Beyond.* New York: Harper & Row, 1971.

Hertog, Thomas. "'I Opened a Bottle with Stephen Hawking to celebrate our eureka moment'—Prof. Thomas Hertog." *Horizon: The EU Research & Innovation Magazine*, interview by Kevin Casey, May 2018.

———. *On the Origin of Time: Stephen Hawking's Final Theory.* London: Transworld, 2023.

"Homo Sapiens." The Smithsonian's Human Origins Program, n.d. https://humanorigins.si.edu/evidence/human-fossils/species/homo-sapiens.

Jansz, Isaac, and Kool, Leonard. *Islam: Een Godsdienst of niet; Deel 1 van 3.* Raleigh, NC: Lulu, 2011.

Kaku, Michio. *Einstein's Cosmos: How Albert Einstein's Vision Transformed Our Understanding of Space and Time.* New York: W. W. Norton, 2005.

Kant, Immanuel. *Metaphysics of Morals.* Translated by John Ladd. Indianapolis: Bobbs-Merrill, 1964.

Kenny, Anthony. *The Five Ways: Saint Thomas Aquinas' Proofs of God's Existence.* New York: Routledge, 2003.

Kierkegaard, Søren. *Concluding Unscientific Postscript.* Translated by Joseph Campbell and Walter Lowrie. Princeton: Princeton University Press, 2019.

Krauss, Lawrence M. *A Universe from Nothing.* New York: Simon & Schuster, 2012

Lehrer, Christopher, and Michel Janssen, eds. *The Cambridge Companion to Einstein.* Cambridge: Cambridge University Press, 2014.

Leiter, Yechiel J. M., *John Locke's Political Philosophy and the Hebrew Bible.* Cambridge: Cambridge University Press, 2018.

Maifreda, Germano. *The Trial of Giordano Bruno.* New York: Routledge, 2022.

Marsico, Katie. *Genius Physist Albert Einstein.* Minneapolis: Lerner, 2018.

McCann, S. M., ed. *Endocrinology: People and Ideas.* New York: Springer, 2013.

McLeish, Tom, and David Hitchings. *Let There Be Science: Why God Loves Science and Science Needs God.* Oxford: Lion Hudson, 2017.

Bibliography

Meadows, Donella H. *The Limits to Growth: A Report for the Club of Rome's Project on the Predicament of Mankind.* New York: Universe, 1972.

Mendel, Gregor Johann. *Experiments in Plant Hybridization: The Genetic Heridity by Hybrids of Garden Pies.* Raleigh, NC: Lulu, 2018.

Mes, G. E. *Bijbelsche Geschiedenis.* Wychen, Netherlands: Erven Kooymans-Mes, 1917. Bible passages concerned translated from Dutch into English by Roger Staats.

"The Milky Way Galaxy." Imagine the Universe!, last edited Dec 2015. https://imagine.gsfc.nasa.gov/science/objects/milkyway1.html.

"New Model of Cosmic Stickiness Favors 'Big Rip' Demise of Universe." Vanderbilt University, Jun 30, 2015. https://news.vanderbilt.edu/2015/06/30/new-model-of-cosmic-stickiness-favors-%E2%80%9Cbig-rip%E2%80%9D-demise-of-universe/.

Newton, Isaac. *The Principia: The Authoritative Translation and Guide; Mathematical Principles of Natural Philosophy.* Berkeley, CA: University of California Press, 2016

Parker, Barry R. *Einstein's Dream: The Search for a Unified Theory of the Universe.* New York: Springer, 2013.

"Potential First Traces of the Universe's Earliest Stars Uncovered." U.S. National Science Foundation, Nov 7, 2022. https://new.nsf.gov/news/potential-first-traces-universes-earliest-stars.

Pritscher, Conrad P. *Re-Opening Einstein's Thought: About What Can't Be Learned From Textbooks.* Leiden: Brill, 2008.

Russell, Randy. "The Solar Furnace." Windows to the Universe, last edited Sep 2, 2010. https://www.windows2universe.org/sun/Solar_interior/solar_furnace.html#google_vignette.

Scotney, John. *The Theory of Evolution.* London: Kuperard, 2010.

Scotti, Paschal. *Galileo Revisited: The Galileo Affair in Context.* San Francisco: Ignatius, 2017.

Seachris, Joshua W. *Exploring the Meaning of Life.* Chichester, UK: Wiley, 2012.

Shakespeare, William. *Hamlet.* Edited by Robert Hapgood. Cambridge: Cambridge University Press, 1999.

Shaver, Peter. *The Rise of Science: From Prehistory to the Far Future.* Cham, Switzerland: Springer Nature, 2018.

Soleyman, Muhammad. *Purpose of Life: An Abjective Approach to Find the Truth.* Independently published, 2021.

Stefan, Viadislav Alexander. *Thus Spoke Einstein on Life and Living.* La Jolla, CA: Stefan University Press, 2011.

Stenger, Victor J. *God: The Failed Hypothesis; How Science Shows That God Does Not Exist.* Amherst, NY: Prometheus, 2010.

Stvarnik, Franjo. *Portraits of the Great Bible-Believing Scientists.* Altona, MB: FriesenPress, 2018.

Tegmark, Mark. *Our Mathematical Universe: My Quest for the Ultimate Nature of Reality.* New York: Vintage, 2014.

Bibliography

Topper, David. *How Einstein Created Relativity Out of Physics and Astronomy.* New York: Springer, 2012.

Tyson, Neil deGrasse (@neiltyson). "Just to Settle It Once and For All: Which Came First the Chicken or the Egg? The Egg—Laid by a Bird That Was Not a Chicken." Twitter, Jan 28, 2013. https://x.com/neiltyson/status/296100559423954944.

———, et al. *Welcome to the Universe: An Astrophysical Tour.* Princeton University Press, 2016.

Warren, Sasha. "How the Earth and Moon formed, Explained." University of Chicago News, n.d. https://news.uchicago.edu/explainer/formation-earth-and-moon-explained.

Wheeler, John Archibald. *Geons, Black Holes, and Quantum Foam: A Life in Physics.* New York: W. W. Norton, 2010.

Wei-Haas, Maya. "Last Day of the Dinosaurs' Reign Captured in Stunning Detail." *National Geographic*, Sep 9, 2019. https://www.nationalgeographic.com/science/article/last-day-dinosaurs-reign-captured-stunning-detail.

Wong, Kate. "The Oldest Homo Sapiens." *Scientific American* 317.3 (September 2017) 12–14.

Zettili, Nouredine. *Quantum Mechanics: Concepts and Applications.* Chichester, UK: John Wiley & Sons, 2009.

Index

Abiogenesis, 35, 39, 58, 139
Abraham, the patriarch, 3, 10, 20
Abrahamic religions, 10, 43–44, 61, 63, 139
Afterlife, 43–46, 51–52, 60, 76–77, 138–39, 145
Agnostic, 23–24, 75, 91, 139
Allah, 10, 17–20, 63
Andromeda nebula, 65, 69
Anselm of Canterbury, 4–5, 145
Aquinas, Thomas. *See* Thomas Aquinas
Aristotle, 6, 48, 54, 146
Artificial intelligence, 67–68
Asteroid, 30, 35, 44, 59, 65–66
Atheist, 23–24, 54, 78, 91, 139
Atom, 15, 32, 34, 39–41, 55, 70, 98, 105, 114–15, 118, 122, 125, 139, 141, 144, 146

Bacon, Francis, 25
Bentley, Richard, 82
Bezos, Jeff, 68
Biden, Joe, 75
Big bang, x, 10–11, 16, 30–34, 38–41, 43, 55–58, 60–61, 71–72, 74, 77, 94, 130–32, 134–37, 139–40, 142, 144
Big bang singularity, 31, 38, 132. 136, 139, 144
Big chill, 70–71
Big crunch, 69, 71, 73

Big freeze. *See* Big chill
Big rip, 70–71
Black hole, x, 38, 44, 65, 76, 101–2, 104, 129–31, 134, 137, 139, 141–42
Body-mind, ix, 23–24
Bohr, Niels, ix, 26, 107, 114–15, 122
Born, Max, 107, 121
Branson, Richard, 68
Broglie, Louis de, 110, 124
Bruno, Giordano, 13

Camus, Albert, 60
Categorical imperative, 25
Christianity, x, 10–16, 19–21, 48, 139
Cogito, ergo sum, 29, 50
Columbus, Christopher, 68
Constants of nature, 55–56, 59, 140–41
Copernicus, Nicolaus, 12–13, 57
Cosmic background radiation, 33, 140
Cosmic calendar, 30–31, 140
Cosmic inflation. *See* Inflation
Cosmological constant, 103, 140
Cosmos, x, 1, 33, 57–58, 140, 143
Creationist, 55, 59, 140

Dark energy, 33–34, 69–70, 73, 76, 140
Dark matter, 33–34, 70, 73, 76, 140

Index

DART (*Double Asteroid Redirection Test*), 65
Darwin, Charles, ix, x, 13–14, 35, 37, 39, 41, 57–58, 66, 85–91, 134, 138, 141, 144
Darwin, Erasmus, 91
Darwin's finches, 89–90
Davies, Paul, 56
Dawkins, Richard, 77
Delft University of Technology, 117
Descartes, René, 6–7, 24–29, 50
Dirac, Paul, 56, 127
Double-slit experiment, 110–13, 116
Dualist, 23, 46–47, 77
Dyson, Frank, 103

$E = mc^2$, x, 34, 97, 105, 131, 144
Eddington, Arthur, 103
Einstein, Albert, ix, x, 33–34, 41, 52, 75–76, 83–84, 92–107, 109–10, 113, 117–18, 120, 127, 129, 131, 133, 138, 140, 142, 144
Einstein equation, 103, 140
Einstein waves. *See* Gravitational waves
Electron, 32, 34, 110, 112–16, 122, 124–25, 127, 133, 139–41, 144
Elementary particle, 114, 116, 118, 121, 126, 133, 140–42, 144–46
Energy, 15, 32, 35, 38, 40–41, 72, 97–98, 101–3, 105, 110, 114, 119–20, 135, 139, 140–42, 144, 146
Entanglement, 117, 141
Entropy, 131, 141, 145
Equivalence, principle 100
Eukaryotes, 35, 141
Event horizon, 129–31, 139, 141
Evolution, 13, 37, 39, 58, 85, 88, 90–91, 134, 141

Feynman, Richard, 128
Fine-tuning argument, 55–56, 72, 141
First law of thermodynamics, 72, 141
First mover, 5, 6
Five ways, 5
Flying spaghetti monster, 77
Four fundamental forces, 76, 98, 118, 133, 141, 146
Freud, Sigmund, 54

Gabriel, the archangel, 2, 9, 17, 19
Galilei, Galileo, 13
General theory of relativity, 34, 38, 99–104, 131, 133, 136, 142, 145
Geodesic, 100, 142
God, ix, 1–11, 16–17, 19–21, 23–24, 27–29, 39–45, 48, 50–53, 55–58, 60–63, 71, 73, 75–78, 84, 91, 106–7, 138–39, 142
Gould, John, 90
Gravitational constant, 55, 82, 140, 142
Gravitational waves, 129–30, 135, 140, 142
Gravity, 99–100, 102–4, 118, 129, 133, 140, 142–43, 146
Greene, Brian, 73, 134
Grossman, Marcel, 103

Hartle, James, 73, 132, 144
Hartle-Hawking model. *See* No-boundary proposal
Hawking radiation, 131
Hawking, Stephen, ix, x, 38, 40–41, 52, 58, 67–68, 72–73, 75, 77, 116, 129–38, 142, 144
Hawking-Hertog new big bang theory, 134–35
Heaven, 52, 62–63, 78, 138–39
Hegel, Georg, 24

Index

Heisenberg, Werner, 114–16, 126, 142
Heisenberg's uncertainty principle, 115–16, 142
Heisenberg's uncertainty relation. *See* Heisenberg's uncertainty principle
Heisenberg's undeterminacy principle *See* Heisenberg's uncertainty principle
Hell, 20, 44, 62–63, 68, 75, 139
Hertog, Thomas, 41, 73, 77, 134–35
Higgs, Peter, 118
Hitchens, Christopher, 77
Hobbes, Thomas, 49
Homo sapiens, 37, 39, 58–59, 66
Hooke, Robert, 84
Hoyle, Fred, 34
Hubble Space Telescope, 75
Hubble, Edwin, 15, 75, 103
Hume, David, 6

Imaginary time, 132, 142
Inertia, 81, 97–98, 143
Institute for Advanced Study, 106
Inflation, 31, 40, 56, 74, 135
Intelligent design, 1, 55, 58, 143
Interference pattern, 111–13
Islam, x, 10–11, 17–21, 45, 63, 139

James Webb Space Telescope, 75
Jesus Christ, 3, 10, 21
Judaism, x, 10, 20, 139

Kant, Immanuel, 5–6, 24–25
Kennedy Space Center, 137
Kierkegaard, Søren, 29
Krauss, Lawrence, 31

Law of gravitation, 79, 81–82, 84, 142
Laws of motion, 81
Leibniz, Gottfried Wilhelm von, 25, 78, 83–84

Lemaître, Georges, 15–16, 94–97
Light year, 44, 130, 143, 145
Locke, John, 25

MacDougall, Duncan, 51
Malthus, Thomas, 66, 85
Mass, 15, 31, 33, 38, 44, 72, 81–82, 97–98, 102–3, 114–15, 117, 129–32, 142–43, 145
Matter, 26, 33–34, 38, 40, 47, 49, 67, 82, 97–98, 101–4, 109–10, 118, 124, 127, 129, 139–40, 142–44, 146
Max Plank Institute for Evolutionary Anthropology, 37
Meaning of life, 60–61
Mendel, Gregor, 14–15, 91
Metaphysics, 26, 143
Milky way, 65, 69, 130
Miller, Stanley, 35
Momentum, 68, 115–16, 126, 133, 142–43
Monist, 23, 46, 48–49, 51, 76
Moses, the prophet, 1–2, 9, 20, 23, 41–42, 53
M-theory, 73, 133, 143
Muhammad, the Prophet, 2, 9–10, 17, 19
Multiverse, 55–56, 72–74, 135, 143
Murphy's law, 71
Musk, Elon, 68

NASA, 32, 57, 65, 136
Natural Science, ix, x, 1, 9, 11, 21, 24, 39–40, 42, 56, 76–78, 107, 142–43
Natural selection, x, 14, 58, 85–89, 141, 144
Naturalist, 55, 143
Neutron, 32, 41, 98, 139, 144–45
New Testament, 21
Newton, Isaac, ix, x, 79–84, 98–99, 102, 104, 107, 110, 113, 136, 138, 142

Index

Nietzsche, Friedrich, 24, 60
No-boundary proposal, 131–33, 144
Nuclear fusion, 32, 144
Nucleus, 34–35, 98, 114–15, 139, 141, 144

Old Testament, 10, 77

Paley, William, 58
Paradise, 19–20, 45, 139
Particle accelerator, 118, 133, 144
Pascal, Blaise, 63
Pauli, Wolfgang, 125
Penrose, Roger, 38
Photoelectric effect, 105, 120
Photon, 41, 110, 114–16, 120, 144
Piketty, Thomas, 66
Pius XII, Pope, 16
Planck constant, 122, 144
Planck, Max, ix, 37, 55, 110–14, 119, 122, 140, 144
Plato, 47
Pope Pius XII. *See* Pius XII
Popper, Karl, 74
Positron, 127, 144
Proton, 31–32, 34, 40–41, 98 139, 144–45
Purgatory, 62, 139
Putin, Vladimir, 52

Quantum fluctuations, 34, 40, 144
Quantum particle. *See* Elementary particle
Quantum physics, ix, x, 26, 33–34, 40–41, 55, 73, 75–76, 105, 107, 108–28, 131, 133, 143–46
Quark, 118, 140, 145
Quasar, 130, 145

Relativity principle, 96
Roman Catholic Church, 11, 47–48
Royal Society, 84, 137
Russell, Bertrand, vi, 60

Sartre, Jean-Paul, 54, 60
Scheler, Max, 54
Scholastics, 27, 50, 145
Schopenhauer, Arthur, 24, 60
Schrödinger equation, 114, 123
Schrödinger, Werner, 114–16, 123
Scientific method, vi, 25, 145
Scripps Research Institute, 35
Shakespeare, William, 78
Singularity, 38, 69, 71, 129, 131–32, 136, 139, 144–45
Socrates, 8
Solvay Conference, 109–10
Solvay, Ernest, 110
Space-time, 38, 101–3, 109, 129, 131, 133, 139–40, 142, 145–46
Special theory of relativity, 92–99, 105, 127, 145
Speed of light, 44, 55–56, 92, 94, 96–99, 117, 140, 144–45
Spencer, Herbert, 88
Spinoza, Baruch, 7–8, 106
Spirit, 43–46, 48, 51, 56, 76–77, 145
Standard model of quantum physics, 118–19, 146
Steinhardt, Paul, 74
Stenger, Victor, 56, 77
String theory, 55, 76, 133–34, 143, 146
Superposition, 116–17, 146
Survival of the fittest, 87–88

Teleportation, 117–18, 146
Ten Commandments, 2, 20, 62
The four fundamental forces. *See* Four fundamental forces
The standard model. *See* Standard model of quantum physics
Theist, 53, 55, 78
Theory of everything, x, 76, 133, 137–38, 146
Theory of evolution. *See* Evolution
Thomas Aquinas, 5–6, 145

Index

Thought experiment, 8, 43, 45, 71–72, 99–100, 109–10, 133
Time dilation, 96, 102, 142–43
Tyson, Neil deGrasse, 88

Universe, x, 8–9, 11–12, 15–16, 30–34, 38–41, 43–45, 51, 54–58, 64–65, 69–78, 98, 103, 107, 117, 130–36, 138–40, 143–46

Unmoved mover, 6
Urey, Harold, 35

Wallace, Alfred Russell, 91
Wave-particle duality, 110, 122, 146
Webb, James, 75
Westminster Abbey, 138
Wheeler, John, 104
Wilde, Jane, 137
Wittgenstein, Ludwig, 22

www.ingramcontent.com/pod-product-compliance
Lightning Source LLC
Chambersburg PA
CBHW060819190426
43197CB00038B/2129